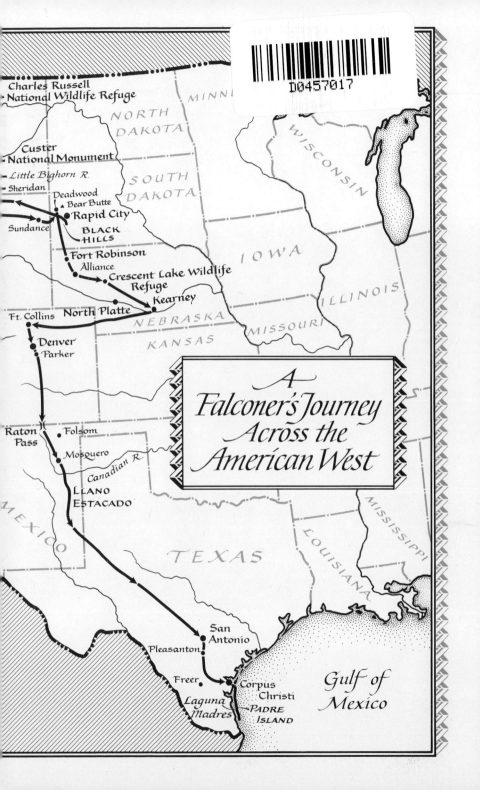

Charles Russell
National Wildlife Refuge

NORTH DAKOTA

MINNE...

WISCONSIN

Custer
National Monument

Little Bighorn R.
Sheridan
Deadwood
Bear Butte
Rapid City
BLACK HILLS
Sundance

SOUTH DAKOTA

IOWA

ILLINOIS

Fort Robinson
Alliance
Crescent Lake Wildlife Refuge
Kearney

MISSOURI

Ft. Collins
North Platte

NEBRASKA

KANSAS

Denver
Parker

Raton Pass
Folsom
Mosquero
Canadian R.

LLANO ESTACADO

MEXICO

A
Falconer's Journey
Across the
American West

TEXAS

LOUISIANA

MISSISSIPPI

San Antonio
Pleasanton

Freer

Corpus Christi
PADRE ISLAND

Laguna Madres

Gulf of Mexico

The RITES of
AUTUMN

ALSO BY DAN O'BRIEN

Eminent Domain
Spirit of the Hills

The RITES of AUTUMN

A Falconer's Journey
Across the American West

DAN O'BRIEN

THE ATLANTIC MONTHLY PRESS
NEW YORK
•

"The Second Coming" reprinted with permission of Macmillan
Publishing Company from *The Poems of W. B. Yeats: A New Edition*,
edited by Richard J. Finneran. Copyright © 1924 by Macmillan
Publishing Company, renewed 1952 by Bertha Georgie Yeats.

Published simultaneously in Canada
Printed in the United States of America

Library of Congress Cataloging-in-Publication Data

O'Brien, Dan, 1947–
    The rites of autumn : a falconer's journey across the American
West / Dan O'Brien.
    ISBN 0-87113-245-1
    1. Peregrine falcon—West (U.S.) 2. Peregrine falcon—West
(U.S.)—Migration.   3. Birds, Protection of—West (U.S.)
4. Peregrine Fund (U.S.) 5. O'Brien, Dan, 1947–   .
6. Birds—West (U.S.) 7. Birds—West (U.S.)—Migration.
I. Title.
QL696.F34037 1988   88-22629   598'.918—dc19

The Atlantic Monthly Press
19 Union Square West
New York, NY 10003

Design by Laura Hough
FIRST PRINTING

This book is dedicated to the thousands of people who contributed to the recovery of the peregrine falcon in North America. And especially to Jim Weaver, who set a standard and taught us why the effort was worthwhile.

The RITES *of* AUTUMN

———————

*F*rom the beginning, the migration of wild things fascinated me. I watched bats in the summer streetlights, diving and twisting for mosquitoes, and wondered where they went after winter killed the insects. Crows and geese would come from nowhere to gather, in the spring and fall, near Lake Erie, and they spoke to me as surely as the stars and the magnetism of the earth spoke to them. They drew me near and I watched them, never knowing exactly why I was watching, but knowing that their wildness was a vital element of life.

Then, on a cool April afternoon in 1965, I watched a peregrine falcon chase sanderlings along a beach of the Gulf of Mexico. It came from somewhere very high and its first stoop was long and flat. I had been watching the sanderlings fly low over the water and noticed when they closed their formation. My previous experience as a bird-watcher allowed me to understand that the sanderlings were "balling up" in response to an aerial attack, but nothing had prepared me for what happened next.

The speed was too much for me to register. There

was only the flat trajectory, the sense that the sander-lings were under attack and the certainty that escape was out of the question. The peregrine was a dark, unfamiliar blur and I could think only that perhaps it was a stray artillery shell or a meteorite that would crash into the waves after it passed through the flock of birds. But it did not plummet into the water. It came out at the bottom of the flock and flared with grace and purpose at the tops of the waves. The air passing through the falcon's wings made a whooshing sound. After its first stoop, the falcon turned on its tail and climbed effortlessly several hundred feet above the rattled sand-erlings. From this position, it controlled them, covering distance in a way that mocked physics. It loomed in the salty air high above, lingered for an instant, then rolled and dove. The second stoop was lethal and the falcon, with a sanderling in its talons, mounted again without so much as a wing flap. In a minute it was gone, leaving just the memory of something alive, moving as fast as imagination allowed, commanding the upper air and, incidentally, the earth below.

Twenty-one years later, sitting on a cliff in the Rocky Mountains, I could see that first falcon as clearly as any of the hundreds I'd seen since. Looking out over the valley below, I marveled at how lucky I had been that day in 1965 to have seen her, because twenty-one years ago falcons were rare indeed, having been poi-soned to near extinction by DDT. In fact, in all of Amer-ica, there were less than twenty known pairs.

I didn't know it then, but at nearly the same time as I saw my first peregrine there were other men and women, standing on other metaphoric beaches, feeling other peregrines steal their imaginations. And gradually, a tiny subculture began to form across the country, a subculture composed of scientists, falconers, ecologists, and hunters, and bound together by the fear that the peregrine falcon might cease to exist. In the years that followed, many of these people sacrificed stable lives, careers, and fortunes in the effort to insure that the peregrine falcon would endure.

Nineteen sixty-five was also the year I received my first communication from the Selective Service, and I rated my chances of sitting on a ledge in Montana near a group of young peregrine falcons much lower than my chances of dying in a rice paddy in Southeast Asia. But that is not the way it worked out. Instead of being drafted, I was hired by The Peregrine Fund, Inc., a nonprofit organization based at Cornell University. Incorporated in 1970, the purpose of the Peregrine Fund was to raise peregrine falcons in captivity and release the young, first on the cliffs of the eastern seaboard, and then in the mountains of the West. My job was to make sure that young falcons raised in the lab were given the best possible chance for survival in the wild. I was responsible for the Rocky Mountains from southern Colorado and Utah to Canada, an area of nearly 500,000 square miles that was originally the home for thousands of peregrine falcons. In 1976, when the Peregrine Fund began its Rocky Mountain work, the entire area held only three known pairs.

Gradually, we had learned to propagate falcons in a laboratory and release them into the wild. In some years nearly a hundred young birds were propagated for release in the Rockies. With an estimated first-year mortality of sixty to seventy percent, about thirty-five young falcons would survive their first year, far more than had been produced in the wild after the heaviest DDT use. Because DDT had been banned and the residues diminished annually, wild peregrines were reproducing again, adding a few young birds to those being released. And by 1986, there were thirty known pairs in the Rockies and the chances of the peregrines' extinction seemed remote. Because of our success, my job was winding down; my life was changing.

All of this ran through my mind as I sat on that ledge in Montana. Beside me was a six-hundred-pound plywood box. Five years before, I had helped sling the box up to the cliff by helicopter, cabling it into place on the ledge. Since then, it had been used as a hack site for releasing peregrines. As I sat looking out over the valley, I could hear four falcons moving inside the box. This was their day to be hacked.

The word "hack" derives from the jargon of ancient falconers. It means, at its simplest, to release. But to anyone with a rudimentary understanding of what is required of a young animal to survive in the wild, the term is filled with incredible optimism and can be viewed as naive or even arrogant in that there is a tendency for people to underestimate what is involved. It has become popular for well-meaning naturalists to create centers dedicated to "hacking back" injured or orphaned birds of prey. Many of these centers feed and care for these birds, even exercise them, until they feel that the bird is ready to be hacked. But there is a flaw in most rehabilitation and hacking programs. The flaw is that they seldom work; an injured or orphaned bird of prey usually becomes a dead bird of prey and the release of such birds, though exhilarating to the rehabilitator, is simply an execution. Birds of prey are fragile. They have evolved so that only the very best survive. (Perhaps as few as ten percent ever make it to breeding age.) The very best are not orphaned; they do not break wings. The very best are perfect and don't need anything that a human can give them except a decent environment. The system that has evolved in nature for the raising and selection of birds of prey is complicated and, in human terms, cruel and severe. The idea that we can improve this system is a classic case of hubris.

Knowing this, our early attempts to release peregrines might have seemed foolish. But the possible extinction of a species is a grave matter, so we had to try. Our goal was to hack falcons in a way that most closely simulated the way they are raised naturally. By studying falcons around nest sites, researching the early falconry literature (falconers of the eighteenth and nineteenth centuries developed methods of hacking young falcons that were re-trapped and used as hunting falcons), a plan was developed that we believed would give falcons we released a reasonable chance of survival.

As humans begin to do certain things, like walk and talk, at certain ages, so do falcons. They begin to eat on their own at about thirty days. They fly at about forty. The peregrines in the hack box beside me were forty-three days old. Eight days before, these falcons had been flown by private airplane to an airstrip close to the hack site. I had picked them up and carried them in a wicker backpack two miles to the top of the cliff. Then

I climbed down a rope to place them in the hack box. For eight days these falcons would live in the hack box, acclimating and readying themselves for freedom. These birds had been raised in a lab. This was their first experience of life in the wild. Like most falcons, they were frightened but docile. In the forty-three days since they were hatched, they had been kept isolated from humans except for a few, unavoidable moments. When I suddenly appeared at the door of the box, they flared the feathers on the back of their heads, rocked back on their tails, feet spread with talons up, and hissed through beaks held open wide. It was the standard menacing posture of birds of prey and, to the uninitiated, it can be intimidating. But it is mostly bluff, designed to give natural predators the impression that these flightless falcons are indeed dangerous.

One by one, I picked up the falcons to fit them with a tiny transmitter, designed to fall off after the first critical week. The large, sluggish female got the blue transmitter. The active male, who struggled in my hands, got the red. The shy male got the yellow and the tough female who made my hand bleed and looked hard into my eyes got the green.

I spread quail on top of and around the box. The falcons were given a liberal supply of food because, after the door to the hack box is opened and the birds come out, they are not disturbed for three days. They need that time to learn how to adjust to their freedom. It would be a minimum of three weeks before they began to catch birds on their own and, until then, they would have no chance for survival without returning to the ledge for food.

8

The
MOUNTAINS

As soon as the quail were distributed, I opened the door. Moving carefully, I quickly snapped my ascenders to the rope, then started up the face of the cliff. Now I had the view that the peregrines would have when they emerged from the hack box. I could not see the ledge. My job was to watch for eagles.

Each hack site has its own problems. Bears, bad weather, and owls are common. At this site the problem was golden eagles. Most people are glad to see golden eagles. With wingspans of nearly eight feet, they are one of North America's largest birds, masters of soaring on the updrafts of mountain ridges and on thermals rising from the prairie. It is commonly thought that these birds are rare, although some biologists believe there are more golden eagles now than ever. In fact, golden eagles nest on nearly every suitable piece of elevated ground in the West and it is not uncommon to see four or five soaring in a single thermal. They are highly successful predators who commonly feed on young deer, antelope, domestic sheep, rabbits, mice, ducks—even peregrine falcons. In fact, in the Rocky Mountains, most of the young falcons that are lost before they reach the age of independence are killed and eaten by golden eagles. And it is against the law to kill golden eagles.

Because of this, I cradled in my lap an old single-barreled shotgun. It was loaded with an exploding shell designed to frighten but not hurt an attacking eagle.

Of course I knew there was really very little I could do to protect the young falcons. Many die and that is unavoidable. But you never get used to it. The term "survival of the fittest" makes perfect sense when read from a college textbook or discussed over coffee, but the reality of it can be demoralizing. Nothing makes you feel more insignificant than to witness a golden eagle swoop down to pluck a clumsy young peregrine falcon from the air. It is a grisly thing to see and only underscores the fact that nature is extraordinarily unforgiving. She is deaf to the peregrine's screams that fade into the whining mountain wind as the eagle disappears over a distant ridge. And even when you think you understand it, when intellectually you see this is the way it has to be, it is still difficult to shrug your shoulders and accept it.

Sitting there, I tried to guess at the order in which the peregrines would emerge. There had been two males and two females. From experience, I knew that the males were more likely to come out first and fly first. I imagined the most active male, the one who had gotten the red transmitter, would come out followed by the green female who had been very aggressive. The smaller, more timid male would not come out for several hours, and the blue female, who was very large and sluggish, I guessed would be last.

By the middle of the afternoon the wind had come up and it was likely that the falcons were now all out of the hack box, strung along the ledge, clutching rocks and grass to hold them down while they beat their wings furiously in mock flight. If the wind kept up, one or two might lift off the ledge and be flying before they knew it.

It was almost dark and I had begun to think of making my way down to the camp when I heard the young falcons begin to kak. The wind had slowed so I heard the kakking clearly. Immediately, I raised the shotgun to a ready position because the sound I heard was the one young peregrines use to signal danger to adults. I scanned the sky, knowing that the falcons could have seen a predator far beyond my vision. The kakking increased. Then I saw a movement, a tiny black spot streaking downward, and I knew it was a golden eagle, stooping at perhaps a hundred miles per hour toward the young falcons. Shouting, I pointed the shotgun at the eagle and pulled the trigger.

It would be wonderful to say that the eagle heard me, that the projectile exploded in his path and diverted it from its prey. But in reality, my voice was lost in the mountain breeze and the projectile exploded two hundred feet behind the eagle. I heard the kakking become frantic and then fade to nothing. For an instant it occurred to me that I had imagined the attack, but of course I had not.

It was dark by the time I got to the camp. Tom and Joyce, my helpers at the hack site, came to meet me and even in the poor light of the Coleman lantern I could see that they were upset. From their position below, they had watched the hack box with binoculars and seen the attack. The story was simple; the eagle had swept in at a terrible speed and taken Yellow as he tried, for the first and last time, to fly. The eagle had simply flown away with him, disappearing from sight a mile down the canyon. Usually, when an eagle has found a place for an easy meal, he will come back. Thus, the three remaining peregrines on the cliff were in danger. The best way to save them was to try to trap them, even though our chances for success were not good. At this stage it is a race with time; could we trap one or two falcons before the eagle got them all? Usually, when an eagle begins to kill young falcons it is too late; you have lost. And even if you trap a falcon, saving it from the eagle, you are beaten. A falcon trapped back from a hack site has lost its opportunity to mature normally and has little chance for survival as a wild bird. The fate of such birds is usually lifelong captivity.

Before I crawled into my sleeping bag, I checked the transmitters, attempting to locate the falcons. Green, the tough female, had fledged before the eagle had appeared; her signal came to me from down the cliff. The slower female, Blue, and the active male, Red, had remained near the hack box. I got no signal at all from Yellow.

Lying in my sleeping bag, I thought about what our approach should be. We would have to try to get down to the box without flushing Blue and Green, set a trap on a dead quail and hope that the falcons were hungry. The lantern hung from a tree not far from where I lay. I got up and turned it off, then crawled back into my bag. The bright white light went yellow and dimmed gradually. Just as it went out I noticed the stars. It would be a cold night for the falcons up on the cliff. But a grand night, cool and crisp. This was the first night they had ever spent outside. They might never see their first migration, but at least they would have a taste of wildness. I could smell autumn on the mountain breeze and my thoughts moved with it.

I fell asleep thinking of the one person in my life who was outside of all this, yet understood, perhaps better than I did myself, why I was here, fighting a battle that meant nothing to most people. It was a question I asked myself often, and it was why I like to think of Kris. She didn't have the doubts I had—she was a doctor and dealt with human lives every day. But somehow she saw what I was doing as important too and seemed to know the answers that I didn't. I lay in my sleeping bag and felt the cold night pressing in on me as I imagined Kris in her warm house in Denver. She would be wondering where I was just then, at that exact moment. I tried to make that my last thought before I fell asleep.

We were up before dawn and ate a cold breakfast. I decided that Joyce would stay at the observation point. Tom would accompany me to the top of the cliff and stand guard while I rappelled to the ledge and set the trap. We set off in the dark, but we were only halfway to the top, the light just bright enough for us to see, when we heard the kakking again.

Forty-five minutes later, as I eased down onto the ledge, I saw there was only one falcon left. It was Blue, the slower female. It is hard to say what qualities best insure a falcon's survival. It is tempting to think that the aggressive, tenacious individuals have the best chance. But in this case, it was possible that Blue's sluggishness kept her quieter than Red and so less attractive to the eagle. I wondered if her luck would hold.

Any extra quail would lessen the chances that a falcon would choose the one in the trap, so I gathered and put into my pack as many quail as I could without disturbing Blue. Out of Blue's sight, I set a trap on a quail, placing it near the front of the box. Blue could see the quail if she moved only a few feet. If she was hungry, she would be caught.

The trap consisted of a wire frame and monofilament nooses designed to snare the toes of feeding falcons. You cannot leave a captured falcon in it for more than a few minutes without risking injury. So, after I ascended, I left my repelling harness still attached to the rope and found myself a niche to sit in where I could see the trap and Blue could not see me. From this position I could reach the trap quickly. I clutched the shotgun and settled into the rocky crevice. I assumed we had lost two falcons, that Red had been plucked from the cliff at first light, which was a little strange because in most cases eagles returned at about the same time of day. But that was if the eagle was hunting only for itself. It was quite possible that this eagle was feeding young. If so, it could be back at any time.

It was almost noon when I heard Blue begin to kak. I looked across the canyon expecting to see an eagle, but it was Green, returning from the place she had spent the night. Her flight was unsure; she flapped her wings at the wrong time and when she came in to land, she toppled forward. Instinctively I looked skyward, knowing that if an eagle had seen Green, it would recognize that she could not escape, and stoop instantly. But no eagle came. Green righted herself and her dignity returned. She jumped onto a rock not far from Blue. She twisted her head upside down and looked at once tame and wild. Suddenly she jumped to a quail I had put in the box the night before and had been unable to remove. It lay on the edge, six feet from the trap. It

14

was bad luck. If she ate her fill she would be impossible to trap.

Green began to pull feathers from the quail, which must have excited Blue, because she flapped over to Green and for an instant they stood over the quail flaring the feathers on the back of their heads. Green tried to carry the quail away but moved only a foot before Blue grasped it with both feet. Green had been the more tenacious of the two when I had handled them in the hack box, but Blue was larger and forced her sister to let go. Green stood in the grass of the ledge, staring fiercely at Blue. It appeared as though she might try to take the quail back but, to my surprise, she suddenly looked to her left and, without hesitation, flew to the quail in the trap. I remained motionless, waiting for her to catch a toe in a noose. She nibbled at the quail, plucking the feathers from it before she ate. Finally I saw her lift one foot and jerk it, flipping it quickly as if annoyed by an insect. She was caught but continued eating. I readied myself to descend, placing the shotgun securely in the crevice.

Years before I had destroyed the hearing in my left ear and so did not hear Tom call to me that the eagle was soaring above. Had my right ear pointed his way I might have heard the warning in time to take up the shotgun and shoot at the eagle. But once I started down it was too late. The eagle was already in full stoop when I saw him. When Green saw both me and the eagle coming, she tried to fly but the trap held her. Blue saw me too and launched into the air. I had to concentrate on securing Green without hurting her, so I did not see Blue struggling to escape the eagle.

An hour later, back at camp, Joyce told us what had happened. Red had been plucked from the cliff at six-fifteen. Apparently, he had not even seen the eagle coming. Blue, after I had frightened her, flew straight for the trees below the cliff, evading the eagle's first stoop, but not the second. The eagle caught her just as she entered the trees. It was over. The eagle could not be blamed.

That site was finished for the year. It would be just as if there had been no attempt to release peregrine falcons in that canyon that year, except that there were three dead falcons, three falcons who would never learn to fly and hunt, never learn if they were good enough to make it, never travel across the face of the continent. And it had been my decision to release them. I had been unable to defend them, so beneath the calm front that I tried to show Tom and Joyce, there was a guilt. I couldn't help thinking that if I had done my job better, if I'd been able to hear Tom's shout, the three falcons would be alive.

I thought about that as I led Tom and Joyce toward the trailhead that afternoon. They carried full packs made heavier by defeat. I carried a light pack and a cardboard box containing the remaining falcon. She was too old to release now. I wondered if it could be said that she had had her chance. I decided that she had not. She would be put into a breeding chamber to live, safe at least, the rest of her life. But as I walked, the guilt came again. Though this falcon would be alive, I could not make myself believe that she would be much better off. The ducks would be gathering soon; most of North

America's birds would be moving within a month. The one in the box should be moving with them. Like falcons born and raised in the wild, she should have the chance to become strong on the wing, to hone her skills on the small birds, to learn to hunt and to kill. She should be able to come down out of the mountains, as wild falcons would, and join the migration on the high plains, and follow it through the unsettled weather of autumn over the grasslands. She should meet the perils of the prairie and, if she survived that, should launch off a piece of gnarled driftwood on the Texas coast and head out across the Gulf of Mexico, to winter where she pleased, far to the south like the rest of her species. And, if all was perfect, to return to her mountain cliff the next spring.

Now she had no chance of survival on her own. Deprived of the natural learning process, there was no chance for her. As I walked, it occurred to me that it was not impossible to teach this falcon some wildness. If done carefully, this falcon might still learn what it needed to survive. It would mean that she would first have to be partially and temporarily tamed and flown as a trained falcon. Somehow she would have to follow the migration like a wild falcon yet be cared for to insure that she got food every day. I tried to shake the idea from my mind as I walked along the bottom of that canyon.

Suddenly, I was tired of reintroducing peregrine falcons and ready for the season to be over. I began to think about getting home, leaving my responsibilities behind. Kris was waiting for me in Denver. And her old

Labrador retriever and my English setter puppy waited for me at my home in South Dakota. I had not seen any of them for five months.

⚘

I left Tom and Joyce in a motel in Bozeman. They were headed for another site in Wyoming. It was the end of my last season with the Peregrine Fund, but still there were a million things to do. I was supposed to be in Utah in two days, but first I had to drive the remaining falcon to our headquarters in Boise. It was a long way and I knew I couldn't drive it that night, but even so I wanted to put some miles behind me before I stopped to sleep. It had been dark for hours and the tourists were off the roads. The hum of the highway beneath the tires of the pickup soothed me and soon I fell into that familiar and pleasant trance that comes with night travel in a motor vehicle. It has occurred to me that this state might be addictive. I know people, and indeed am one myself who, when things aren't going exactly right, feel the need to jump into a pickup and drive several hundred miles in one direction or the other.

For thirty miles I thought about that. I was driving through some of North America's wildest country, land that had a history of inspiring men to travel to it and within it. This was the land of mountain men. There were no great fortunes made by the men who roamed these mountains, no quick fame, and no great sense of patriotism made them travel those hazardous paths. In fact, it is hard to imagine what impulse drove men like John Colter and the rest of the early trappers. When you realize that most of the mountain men died violently, it's difficult to understand why they chose the lives they did. Because these men were not literate, we have little of their thoughts on the matter. The only indication of their reasoning that came to my mind that night was in the name that they chose to describe themselves. Free Trappers they called themselves. American Free Trappers. Free.

That night, passing Three Forks—the confluence of the Jefferson, Madison, and Gallatin Rivers, the genesis of the Missouri—the stories came back to me. Colter was born in Virginia, to a landowning family, about 1774. There is no record of him before he turned up in Maysville, Kentucky, at the age of about thirty. That was in 1803 and Kentucky was the frontier. Colter had walked there from Virginia to answer a newspaper advertisement asking for "a hundred strong young men, accustomed to living out-of-doors," for an expedition up the Missouri River.

Colter met Captain Meriwether Lewis in Maysville. Captain Clark joined them in St. Louis. A year and a half later they found themselves in the same country I drove through the night after the eagle attack.

The information is sketchy, but on their return trip, at a Mandan village in what is now North Dakota, Colter alone was discharged from his obligations with the expedition. He was given all the equipment the expedition could spare, and he promptly returned to the headwaters of the Missouri, the area I traveled through that night. Floating down the Missouri to St. Louis with Louis and Clark, he acquiesced to the pull of life in the wilderness. It is the only context that we know him in, as if he never existed in the civilized world. He did return to St. Louis when he was about forty, but no one remembers what he did there. He is remembered as an Indian fighter, an explorer, a beaver trapper, and an entrepreneur of the early fur trade. But there is only one report where Colter is said to have killed an Indian. If he was an explorer, he was the kind who didn't document his explorations in any way. Though he traveled with beaver trappers, he seemed to prefer guiding and hunting to the actual trapping, and for all his hardships he retired with nearly nothing to show for his years in the fur trade.

Colter was the first white man to see what is now Yellowstone National Park. He left the confluence of the Big Horn and Yellowstone Rivers and walked a circle, mostly in the winter, around Yellowstone, as far south as Jackson Hole, and returned to the Big Horn after walking over five hundred miles alone through unknown country. He was the first man to explore the Three Forks area, the territory of the Blackfeet, and several times narrowly escaped with his life. Even the famous incident when he was stripped naked and chased by eight hundred armed Blackfeet, as a sort of test, could not keep him from his chosen life-style. Why did Colter do these things? What could make an intelligent young man, from a middle-class background, leave his home to roam an extremely dangerous and unknown country without recording any of what he saw? There is no evidence that John Colter was interested in fame or profit. Yet in my driving trance that night, it made perfect sense. To stop, for Colter, was to cease to exist. The great risks were beside the point.

John Colter was defined by his movement, his freedom. It seemed no fluke to me that within three years of the day Colter surrendered his life-style, he was dead.

I would like to have known the John Colter of the Three Forks area, would like to have shared a camp with him on the Big Horn or walked beside him as he passed the wonders of Yellowstone. But I would not like to have been his neighbor after he retired and settled as a farmer in Missouri and slowly turned yellow with jaundice and died. I reached out in the pale light from the pickup's dashboard and touched the box that held the peregrine falcon. Any definition of John Colter should begin with "the man who roamed the Yellowstone country." That, more than his height, weight, religious beliefs, or parents, defined John Colter. Without it, the man was not John Colter. And a peregrine falcon, I thought, was more than a blue-black, crow-sized bird of prey. Much more important was "the wanderer, the bird that stoops with more speed and grace than any other." I reasoned that a bird with a broken wing, by definition, is not a peregrine. A bird in a cardboard box in the front seat of a pickup truck was not a peregrine either.

I was thinking about this as I pulled onto Interstate 15 just north of Dillon, Montana. It was very late and I felt suddenly exhausted. By the time I reached Monida Pass I began to experience hallucinations. Suddenly, it began to seem important that the falcon in the box be given the chance to become what its genes had prepared it to be. And it occurred to me that it would be a necessary privilege for me to go along. It was true that my job was temporary and that things would slow down enough in a few weeks that my services would not be missed. But it was also true that I had obligations on my land in South Dakota and that the federal and state permits to allow me to travel with a falcon on a natural migration path would be expensive and very difficult to obtain. But, I reasoned with myself, my obligations in South Dakota could be put off another month, the permits procured as required. If I could get permission from the federal authorities and the state of Montana, I could at least begin.

At the top of the pass I found the gravel road that I had slept on before. There was no need to pull off the road too far, just enough so that headlights of the few cars that might pass would not sweep over me as I lay at the edge of the sagebrush. When I turned the engine off and stepped out, the night seemed dark and cold. But as my eyes grew used to the moonlight, I could see a surprising distance. The sagebrush cast three-dimensional shadows on itself and a slack strand of barbed wire ran, doubled by the moonlight, into silver-green infinity. I rolled a foam pad and a sleeping bag onto the grass beside the truck, and slipped a pistol under the pad where my head would be. Then I went to the truck and slid into the cab beside the cardboard box.

The box was standard issue for moving young peregrines. Like much of the material and equipment used in the recovery effort, it was donated to the cause. This box had the name of a moving company on the side. Though I knew that cardboard was the best material for transporting falcons because it was safe for feathers and talons I had never gotten used to the ignoble way here and there, all finally heading toward the Gulf of Mexico. But by the time I settled into my sleeping bag and closed my eyes, flocks of lark buntings whirred along the fence lines of my mind, Canada geese honked above, and all of us moved steadily southward in front of the huge cloud bank that was winter.

The
NORTHERN
PLAINS

I came home late on a Tuesday night. There was a cattle sale on Friday and Erney, the friend who works for me with little pay, needed help loading the heifers. We had not seen each other for months and, even though we had talked on the telephone often, there was a lot to catch up on. I told him about the summer releasing peregrines and he told me about putting up hay and the knives he was making from Damascus steel. Jake, Kris's old Labrador retriever, lay with his head against my boot and Spud, my fourteen-month-old setter, sat a few feet away twisting his head as if trying to understand the talk. Erney told me there had been thirteen male sharp-tailed grouse on one dancing ground and six on the other. The mallards on the ponds were feathered out. He had seen twenty-three antelope in the back pasture. And then later, after the pot of coffee was gone and the whiskey had come out, he asked about the peregrine falcon I had begun to call Dolly.

I brought her into the kitchen and we examined her under the pale light. In Boise, another friend, Bill Heinrich, had helped me take her from the free-flight chamber where she had been kept until the reintroduction season ended. We fitted her with traditional light-weight falcon bells, and soft leather bracelets on each leg with grommets to hold removable straps that are called jesses. Bill had made a hood for her and, in the manner of ancient falconers, she had remained hooded for two days while she traveled, to protect her from the trauma of new, frightening sights. Now in the kitchen of the small ranch house, after examining her feathers, feet, talons, and general shape, the hood came off. She stood on my fist, surprised by the light and the humans staring at her, but her eyes remained defiant and both Erney and I were riveted with their wildness. After only a few seconds, I slipped the hood back on and tightened the braces by pulling them with my right hand and teeth because my left hand was occupied supporting the falcon. When she was hooded again we didn't say anything for a long time. We looked at her and then at each other with knowing, excited grins.

The next day I dug out a laminated maple and walnut perch built like a small solid bongo drum with an iron spike at the bottom that pushed into the ground and a swiveling top of soft astro turf to protect the falcon's feet. I had made the perch sixteen years before. Originally there had been five of them, all made at the same time and intended to last the rest of my life. The one that I dug out of the mass of dog harnesses, pack saddles, and clay pigeon launchers was the last of the bunch. I had given the rest, like some of the falcons that had stood on them, to young men whom I thought would put them to good use. This last falcon block seemed massive by current standards. In recent years, falconry equipment in the United States has become extremely fine. The block that I pushed into the earth of the weathering yard at the ranch had been state of the art in its day and, even though it was old and the swivel mechanism a little crude, it looked magnificent with a peregrine standing on it.

During the two weeks I stayed at the ranch, Dolly, when she was not on my fist, lived in the weathering yard, safe from predators. At first, to insure that she would not get overly excited and hurt herself, she remained hooded, except at night and when she was fed. After a few days I allowed her to sit unhooded, leashed to the block for short periods of time. As she became accustomed to Erney and me, I extended the time she was left unhooded and introduced her to things like automobiles and horses. The object was to expose her to different things gradually so that she would not become frightened and try to fly away. Attempting to fly away, and so coming suddenly to the end of the leash, is called "bating," and it is something to be avoided. The process of the falcon becoming used to man and his activities is called "manning." For falcons that are intended for normal use in falconry, the more complete the manning, the tamer and better they will be. In Dolly's case the approach had to be different. She had to be sufficiently used to men and dogs to not be traumatized at the sight of them, but still aloof enough to revert quickly to a wild state when I released her. Dr. Tom Cade, founder of the Peregrine Fund and author of *Falcons of the World*, describes falconry as a specialized form of bird-watching. If he is right, and I believe he is, it stands to reason that one of the purposes of falconry is impression the boxes created. They seemed so makeshift; I would have preferred something more like the boxes made for fine jewelry. But I was dreaming. I slowly moved my eye to one of the air holes cut along the top of the box so that I could check the peregrine's condition without disturbing it. But the interior of the box was dark and when my eye finally adjusted, I found that I was the one who was being observed. She looked up at me, and her deep brown eyes reflected the moonlight. She did not seem frightened, but aloof, superior, and her stare made me feel insignificant. There was no hate. If there was a human equivalent for what I saw in that falcon's eyes, it was pity. She made me look away.

I sat on the seat of the pickup with the door open and my hands draped over the steering wheel. To the south the sky was shotgunned with stars. After a minute, the stars began to take their familiar forms; soon I could see Orion, the hunter, staring down at me like a hopeful father. It could be done, I thought. And, oh, what a trip! Freedom by association, I said. Then I shook my head. No, it couldn't work. Simulating the experiences needed for the falcon to survive would be impossible. Men were not built for that kind of dispassion. It was the long drive and mountain air that made it seem possible.

But the idea of following the migration, seeing it the way the young falcon in the cardboard box might see it, would not leave me. As I got ready to slide into the sleeping bag, I saw the world as I had seen it that morning from the top of the cliff, the way the peregrine sees it, stretching out in river systems that wind their to keep the falcon performing very much like a wild falcon, only compromising those wild traits that could be harmful to the falcon in its new situation.

I spent as much time as I could lying in the grass near Dolly in those two weeks. I read old, familiar books and thought about the connection between her species and mine. Peregrines and men have a special history, a tradition of association rivaled by only two other animals, the horse and the dog. But the peregrine stands apart because it has never been domesticated. (It is indeed a little sad to think that the recent achievements in captive breeding of birds of prey might change that.) Though the degree to which a horse or dog has forsaken its ancestral ways determines its attractiveness to mankind, the opposite could be said of the peregrine. Yet there is that special undeniable tie. No one has captured the essence of the peregrine-human relationship as well as Rodger Tory Peterson in *Birds Over America*. "Man has emerged from the shadows of antiquity with a Peregrine on his wrist. Its dispassionate brown eyes, more than those of any other bird, have been witness to the struggle for civilization, from the squalid tents on the steppes of Asia thousands of years ago, to the marbled halls of European kings in the seventeenth century." And now, I thought, witness to twentieth-century North American man struggling to understand his relationship to, and place within, his environment.

Why the peregrine? I asked myself. The question was rhetorical. I knew the answer; it was in my head and in the books and papers I had brought out to browse through as I spent time with Dolly. The peregrine's power over man's imagination lies in its ability to inspire. They are beautiful in an understated way. The adults have blue-black backs of tiny feathers, each with its own gradation of color, and broad breasts of white salmon, speckled with dark spots. I looked at Dolly in her dark immature plumage and took special note of her bluish yellow feet, the long slender toes, and the ebony talons. She raised a foot just then and scratched the tiny feathers under her chin as delicately as a lady might scratch her nose at a dinner party. Still holding the foot up, she tugged gently at the small bell attached to her leg. Then she turned her stare directly on me and those dark eyes came right inside. If the eyes are the window to the soul, the peregrine's soul is deep and awesome. There are wild rivers in those eyes, mountains, oceans, and the speed and will to bring them all into the peregrine's sphere. They nest in the most beautiful places on earth. In the days of their rapid decline, when peregrine nests were few and very hard to find, it was commonly known that the best way to find a peregrine eyrie was to go to the nearest tourist trap and look at the postcards of local places of beauty. The rocks and spires, the panoramas and sweeps of landscape that attracted the photographer, had usually attracted the peregrine years, perhaps centuries, before. In Colorado in the early 1970s, most of the remaining peregrine falcon eyries could be found pictured on any revolving display of postcards.

Peregrines and people seem to have the same aesthetic taste. Twice I have been on falcon research trips and had a companion turn to me with a slight shake of the head and a faraway look in his eye and say, "They sure know where to live." The first time that happened was on the top of a cliff overlooking the tundra of Greenland. The second was on an offshore island in the Gulf of Mexico. There are countless other aesthetic ties. Peregrines and falconry are mentioned in the works of scores of poets: Byron, Browning, Coleridge, Keats, and Yeats, to name a few. There are literally hundreds of falconry allusions and metaphors in the works of Shakespeare. "Hood my unmann'd blood, bating in my cheeks," (*Romeo and Juliet*, iii, 2) is one of many examples of Shakespeare's synthesis of interhuman emotion and the emotion produced by man's interaction with the wildness and beauty of falcons.

And in the eclectic pile of books and papers that I had hauled out was a battered copy of a Yeats poem. Once again I turned to "The Second Coming," a poem I have never been able to understand, and read it aloud as if Dolly might be able to help me. It begins:

> *Turning and turning in the widening gyre*
> *The falcon cannot hear the falconer;*
> *Things fall apart; the center cannot hold:*
> *Mere anarchy is loosed upon the world,*

Yeats has chosen the loss of the falcon to trigger the second coming, but not of the Christ that many expect:

> *And what rough beast, its hour come round at last,*
> *Slouches toward Bethlehem to be born?*

A week later, I drove westward with the dogs and the falcon in the back of my truck and Erney in the passenger seat. There was something in me that did not want to leave the ranch, that wanted to walk around my 760 acres of dry pasture every morning for the rest of my life, to get to know the neighbors again and buy a quarter horse colt to work with on a daily basis. But by then Dolly was ready to go, and the federal permit had come through. I was committed.

We were headed toward the Charles M. Russell National Wildlife Refuge. That, and the land north of it to the Milk River has always been special for me. It is isolated and wild—the plains of North America—but with mountains in almost every direction. This land abounds with wildlife and is populated by people who seem more respectful of this land and more in love with it than people in other places. Cool weather comes early in this part of the country. In September waterfowl begin to bunch up on the ponds, passerines gather by the thousands in the woody draws, and falcons and hawks slide down the surrounding mountain slopes to feed on them. In addition to the migrants, there are residents: sage grouse, sharp-tailed grouse, magpies, and partridge. The days are warm and breezy, the nights can have a touch of frost in them, the choke cherries begin to turn blood red.

The pickup was loaded to its limit. The bed was covered by a fiberglass camper shell with a heavy metal rack on the top for extra cargo. Under the shell, on one side of the bed, we had built a special perch for Dolly. Along the other side was a set of built-in cupboards where we stored cooking gear, a Coleman stove, and extra clothing. Jake and Spud had beds that were thrown on top of our sleeping bags, boxes of books, and a flat plastic gun case holding two shotguns and a rifle.

Strapped on top of the camper were the big things: my tent—eight feet by twelve feet when set up, a wood-burning stove, and the food box. In the cab, behind the seat, was a mixture of falconry equipment: a hunting bag, scale, block, bath pan. Erney and I were a little crowded.

Erney had never been to the plains of northern Montana and he was looking forward to seeing them. Now forty-six, he had seldom been out of South Dakota. He grew up speaking Czechoslovakian in an isolated community in eastern South Dakota. Although his formal education ended after high school, and he had worked as a laborer most of his life, he read constantly and had a great knowledge of the natural world. As we traveled, I asked him questions. What kind of trees are those? Why doesn't grass grow on those hills? And he would tell me. He had read about it, he said, but this was the first time he had actually seen the things that we talked about.

We crossed the sagebrush flats of northeastern Wyoming between the Black Hills and the Big Horn Mountains. It had been a good summer in that area; the sagebrush and grass were greener than usual. There were antelope by the hundreds, grazing in small bands on both sides of the road. Their kids, usually twins, could still be distinguished from their mothers by size. Occasionally we would pass a band of young bucks or a single, large male standing on a high spot looking as majestic and exotic as anything Africa has to offer.

Tucked beneath the shoulders of the Big Horn Mountains, Sheridan, Wyoming, is one of the most beautiful places in the West. There are no foothills on this eastern frontier of the Rocky Mountains. Here the sagebrush flats meet the mountains abruptly and the land rises thousands of feet, giving the impression of a wall thrown up in the traveler's path. The Big Horns are the beginning of the Rockies. Even in September, the snow-capped peaks tower above the sagebrush prairie. This is an ecological transition zone, incredibly fertile for wildlife. Within easy driving distance of Sheridan, there are elk, two kinds of deer, bear, antelope, several kinds of grouse, partridge, pheasants, ducks, and countless varieties of small mammals and birds. Because of this, there are more falconers per capita in Sheridan than any other town in the United States, and it feels a little like home to me.

We pulled into Dan and Jeannie Konkel's drive-way in the afternoon, just in time to block Dolly in their weathering yard and watch Dan fly his new gyrfalcon. Dan and Jeannie were old friends. The three of us had spent their honeymoon hawking sharp-tails in South Dakota. Later, they gave up jobs in the Denver area and moved to Wyoming to raise gyrfalcons. Gyrfalcons are arctic birds but adapt well to the northern plains where they are often seen in the dead of winter. They are the largest falcons in the world and one of the most beautiful, with plumage that varies from a smoky black to pure white. Dan specializes in raising these falcons and produces lovely light-colored birds that weigh nearly four pounds, twice the size of peregrines. The gryfalcon Dan flew that day was a bird of the year who was just learning to hunt. When he brought her out I shook my head at the size of her. She was massive; Dan had aptly named her Jabba the Hut. As with all falcons, female gyrfalcons are a third larger than the males. Knowing that Jabba was intended to be used eventually as a breeder, I felt sorry for any male that would have to deal with her. But as it turned out, Dan had raised her with only human contact so she was imprinted. She thought that she was a person and treated Dan as her mate. This gave new meaning to the term "henpecked."

We drove to the outskirts of the town with Jabba and Dan's dog, Lance, in the back of Dan's truck. Lance is a beautiful setter, a son of the famous dog Jet Train, the grandson of Tomoka, and he had been given to me several years before, when my situation would not allow another dog. So I had given him to Dan and Jeannie.

To the north of Sheridan the land rolls in long treeless valleys of sage and native grass. There are sharp-tails and sage grouse in the coulees and sage flats. The last time I had hunted there was with another friend, and his peregrine had killed a teal that had come off one of the stock ponds dotting the country. The ponds were full with run-off from the wet summer, perfect for attracting ducks. But today we were looking for bigger game. There are only a few birds that are large enough and fast enough to test a gyrfalcon like Jabba. The sage grouse, which weighs up to seven pounds, is one of them. Sage grouse are extremely fast once they get going, and they live in country that is open and relatively flat. Pointing dogs love them because they are easy to scent and hold well before flushing.

Lance knew where he was and exploded from the back of the truck. He started down a coulee, but Dan called him back and made him sit while he got Jabba ready to fly. He removed the kangaroo-hide jesses (straps eight inches long and a half-inch wide) from the bracelets around Jabba's legs. Then Dan attached a tiny transmitter to Jabba's leg, in case she became lost, and after lifting her on his left fist, he waved Lance out with his free hand. And we began to walk, the three of us abreast, moving through the native grass, smiling now, and watching the setter casting out along the edges of the coulees, running to get downwind of likely patches of sage.

Watching a good bird dog is soothing. You can see in the way it holds its head and tail high that it enjoys what it does. There is a sense of excitement about the way a bird dog moves. The dog's genetic essence has been aroused. Now, free of the kennel, he is doing what he has been bred to do. And, what is more, he is doing it with what he must perceive as his pack. To Lance, we were hunting together, coordinating our efforts to catch and kill game. It is the way all dogs see their lives, as part of a pack that consists of the people and dogs with whom they live. Lance checked back over his shoulder occasionally to see that his hunting partners were still coming. He ran and hunted the way that I hoped Spud would someday. At fourteen months Spud was still too playful to hunt seriously and, though he had shown signs of a good nose and a willingness to point, he would have been a liability in the highly coordinated interaction between pointing dog and falcon. This afternoon belonged to Lance and Jabba.

After a few minutes, Lance disappeared into a deep coulee. When he came up the other side, he moved slowly, his tail whipping excitedly. Dan stopped to watch. "He's making birds," he said. We watched as Lance assumed a low crouch, moving parallel to the wind. He swung into the wind, hesitated, moved on and finally froze, tail solid and perpendicular to his back. "There they are," Dan said.

No one moved. We watched Lance for another instant to be sure he had located the grouse, and then Dan took the hood off Jabba. She had been sitting calm and relaxed, but when the hood came off, her feathers slicked down and her black eyes, even more piercing against her almost white feathers, fixed on the horizon and on the dog frozen just at the top of the next hill. She let all her feathers go limp, then realigned them with a shake that falconers call a "rouse." When the feathers were back tight against her body she launched into the breeze. Now we waited, hoping that she would take a high pitch above the setter and the grouse hidden in front of him.

The breeze carried her fifty yards behind us. She banked and pumped powerfully into the wind. Gyrfalcons lack the grace and love for flying that are the hallmarks of the peregrine, but they are masters of power flying. Once she turned into the wind, Jabba gained several feet of altitude with each wing flap. Since it is rare for a gyrfalcon to catch a grouse without a height advantage, Dan waited until Jabba had improved her pitch. Then we moved slowly to a position just behind Lance and waited until Dan decided that Jabba's position gave her the best chance for success.

There is a trick to watching a flight at grouse. Unless you are a long way from the flush, you shouldn't try to see it all because too many things happen too fast for the human eye to take in. To get even the barest notion of what is happening, it is best to concentrate on either the falcon or the grouse. I watched the grouse.

Dan walked past Lance, restraining him with a soft "Whoa." When Jabba was in position above them, I heard Dan rush forward and then the wonderful kuk kuk kuk of flushing grouse. Jabba rolled and dropped vertically downward. The grouse was an old cock, large and wise, no doubt the successful escapee of several attacks by wild falcons. It flew with its neck and tail extended; its wings beat in bursts of four or five rapid flaps, then a glide. The old bird watched the falcon as she stooped. Just as Jabba closed on him, he rolled sideways without missing a wing beat and, as a result, the sound that we heard was only the sound of the falcon's wing hitting that of the grouse. Jabba's talons never came close, and though she recovered from her stoop and chased him, the grouse escaped with ease.

We waited for fifteen minutes while Jabba, angry that she missed the grouse, flew back and forth on the horizon a mile away. She was probably searching the draw where the grouse disappeared, although there was no possibility of her finding it. When she came back she was still mad, as if she thought Dan had not flushed the grouse at the right time. She slammed into the lure that Dan swung on its long line and tore at the meat attached as if it were the grouse that had beaten her. She screamed hatefully for a time, but after a few minutes she seemed to forgive us and stood on Dan's fist calm and happy. Erney and I moved closer and watched Jabba clean her beak on Dan's glove. Dan thought it was a good lesson for her and that she would be a little smarter the next day. She received only enough food to appease her anger and was still hungry when she was hooded. She could now think about what she might have done to secure a whole grouse.

Interstate 90 connects Sheridan, Wyoming, with Billings, Montana, and the high plains beyond. It heads north along the Little Big Horn River to Crow Agency, a small town not far from what is called Custer Battlefield. When I think of the battle itself, my mind skips over the accounts of both cavalrymen and Indians and settles on something that Neihardt extracted from several who were there and set down in this book *Black Elk Speaks*. On the day of the battle, thousands of Indians swam in the Little Big Horn River that flowed through their camp. The juxtaposed images of these native people at ease and, in fact, immersed in the environment, and the stiff sweating troopers of the 7th Cavalry fighting every mile of that prairie, are jarring. It is the enigma of Montana, the old and the new. Harmony and discord with the landscape. Custer Battlefield National Monument is located at one of the gateways to the state. Every year thousands stop there to remember the troopers and the Indians who died. But to many it stands as a monument to something very different, something ugly, something that is still very much alive.

Past Billings, we turned up Highway 87 toward Roundup, Lewistown, and the old open-range cattle country of the Judith Basin. Now we were anxious to set up camp and prepare Dolly for her first free flight. We entered the Charles Russell National Wildlife Refuge just as we came to the top of the bluff overlooking the Missouri River. The river meandered in a silver band below us, and already the cottonwoods along the Missouri had begun to show some gold. The hint of color reminded me again that it was time we were in camp, time Dolly was on the wing.

Signs of the wet summer were everywhere. The grass was particularly tall for September, the sage a deeper silver-green, and the dirt roads heading to the Robinson ranch house were cut deep with hardened ruts. We were offered coffee by Mrs. Robinson but refused. We talked about all the rain that they had had, and finally Mr. Robinson said that he'd come along with us to the campsite. We followed his big four-wheel-drive pickup along a new road to a point where I had camped in years past. The road that we had used before had been washed out by the summer rains and Mr. Robinson wanted to be sure we found the new way. Actually we would have had no trouble, but he wanted to go along. The closest town of any size was fifty miles away and the prospect of conversation must have appealed to him.

I let the dogs out and blocked Dolly under the only tree for miles. While Spud and Jake investigated the vicinity and Dolly preened, the three of us unpacked my truck. We talked more about the unusual summer weather, the price of cattle, the possibility of another grain embargo, and the chance of an early winter. Before Mr. Robinson left, he told us to stop by for coffee or "just to visit."

We pitched the tent just below the dam of a stock pond. The idea was to shield ourselves from the northwesterly winds without camping in the bottom of a coulee that might flood during a freak storm. The spot we chose was matted with buffalo grass and surrounded by sagebrush. There was a little water in the coulee for the dogs and Dolly could be blocked under the gnarled cottonwood for shade yet still have a grand view of the country below us. We built a rough table fifteen feet from the tent, set the wash pan and the falcon scale on an old wooden box, and put the folding chairs near the tent flap. Inside the tent, a cot was set up along each wall; our wood-burning stove went between them. I hung a lantern from a wire wrapped around the ridge pole.

By dark we were settled in. The dogs had been chained to keep them from wandering. Pork chops and potatoes fried in the skillet. Dolly had been carried for an hour before she was put away in the truck for safety. She had been given nothing to eat in preparation for the next phase of her training, which would begin in the morning. Erney and I, wrapped in wool sweaters against the chill of the night, settled into folding chairs with our plates full. We didn't speak. The dogs lay quietly not far away, but when we heard the first coyote, the puppy's head rose with a snap. If he had heard coyotes before, it had been from inside the ranch house in South Dakota. These Montana coyotes must have seemed very close. He stared into the dark and then at us. Still we said nothing. We glanced at each other and smiled and finally Spud put his head back down. But I doubt that he slept much. I wonder how much sleep any of us got that night. The men, the dogs, the falcon; I wonder if we thought the same thoughts, heard the same sounds, anticipated the morning with the same sense of wonder.

An hour after we turned in, a light rain began. I got up, in just my shorts, and put the dogs in the back of the pickup with Dolly. The night was dark, and the rain made the air feel thick and heavy. I was chilled and damp when I crawled back into my sleeping bag. My mind was filled with tiny details, mostly about starting Dolly the next day. I had reduced her weight over the past week and she now trusted me enough to jump a few feet to my fist for food. Tomorrow we would fly her to the lure, a light leather bag with food attached tied at the end of an eight-foot cord. The lure is swung around the falconer's head to attract a falcon, then allowed to fall to the ground where the falcon feeds on it. At first Dolly would be tied to a fifty-foot line called a creance, in case she should try to fly away. Later she would be flown free to the lure. This was an important stage in the training. If it went well, she would be off the creance in a few days, chasing game in a week. That is the image I took with me to sleep.

But at two o'clock I was again awakened by the rain. This time it was driven by a powerful wind. The canvas of the tent snapped, and I could feel the floor rising under my cot. The wind came in gusts, and it seemed to be increasing in velocity. I lay awake for perhaps half an hour, the wind whistling through the seams of the tent and the snapping of the canvas becoming more violent. I was afraid the wind might tear the tent or bend the aluminum poles.

"You awake, Erney?" I finally said.

"Yep." It was a silly question. No one could sleep with wind howling and whipping the tent like that.

The tent bent with the gale; the windward pegs had been pulled up and the corners flapped furiously. The aluminum frame, on which the tent was hung, was under a terrible strain, and it was clear that the only thing keeping the tent from blowing away was our weight.

"It must be blowing fifty miles per hour," I said over the din.

"At least," Erney said. "Better tie her down."

Because of the danger that the tent might blow away, we decided that Erney should stay where he was. Waiting for a lull, I sat on the edge of the cot and pulled on some clothes. When the lull came, I lunged out of the tent and through the needlelike rain to the pickup, which I moved to the windward side of the tent. Even the pickup was buffeted by the wind, and the rain sounded like BBs thrown in handfuls against the windshield and roof. I was soaked before I finished tying the tent to the camper but took an extra moment to look into the back of the pickup. The dogs were curled tightly; Dolly's head was tucked behind a wing, and she stood peacefully on one leg. It was as if the storm didn't matter to them.

But the storm was still at full force. The tent still rocked and popped but now it remained upright. Freezing cold, I stripped my clothes off and climbed into the sleeping bag. For an instant I had the feeling that the goose down would somehow keep the cold in and I would freeze to death in my bag like a climber on a cliff face. But soon warmth crept back into my arms and legs. Erney snored peacefully. But I did not sleep. I had been affected by Dolly's calmness in the back of the pickup. I wondered if her reaction would have been different if she had been wild and on the first leg of a real migration. I wondered if she would have been as calm if she had been settled in a dwarfed prairie tree when the storm had hit. Would she have been frightened then? As frightened as I had been? Or would she still feel at ease, content, with a harmony that had proved impossible for me?

The weather stayed wet for three days, which suited our purposes. Sunny days tend to make a falcon want to fly, not just on the end of a creance but soaring to heights that are beyond the vision of man. Nice weather also makes falcons think that food is not important because they don't need as many calories. So I was glad for the gray days.

Dolly came to the lure the first time she saw it. It was the morning after the storm and the sage flats were soaked. Large shallow puddles stood on the hard pan. The wheat grass was bent over, holding water like sponges. I put Dolly on a fence post, tied to the creance. When she saw the coturnix quail attached to the lure, she jumped neatly into the wind, flapping her wings only twice, then gliding in neatly with the creance dragging behind. She clutched the lure as if it might try to get away, then began to eat. She had flown only fifteen feet, not much of a flight, but it was a start.

I was tempted to try it again, but I resisted,

knowing that one good experience was more valuable than ten mediocre ones. I sat in the wet grass, watching her eat. She weighed twenty-eight ounces that morning. I did not want her to gain more than a quarter of an ounce. The quail on the lure, plus the little bit of meat I would need to get her on my fist, had been calculated to keep her at twenty-eight ounces. If the temperature remained about the same, she would be ready to fly again the next morning. When she finished the quail on the lure, there was an instant when she was confused and did not realize there was more food on my glove. I extended my fist toward her, and she looked up and around as if she might try to fly. The end of the creance was in my hand so there was no chance of her escaping, but if she flew I would have to restrain her and the training would suffer. I froze, then slowly wiggled the meat in my gloved hand. As soon as she saw it, she relaxed and stepped onto the glove to finish her meal. Then, to get her used to different sights and the feeling of riding on my hand, we walked for an hour before I hooded her. There had been a few days a week earlier when she had seemed to resent the hood, but now she took it well. She stood at ease, her eyes level with mine, and raised the nictitating membrane over her eyes as the hood came up. The hood's main function is to keep the falcon calm, and Dolly had learned that once the hood was on she was safe and could relax.

Our camp was situated in the middle of thousands of acres of sagebrush pasture. Some of the land belonged to private ranchers, but most was public, managed by the BLM and leased to the local people at nominal rates to supply summer range for their cattle. It is a kind of government subsidy for part of the cattle industry. Occasionally, I lease land from my neighbor in South Dakota, paying fifteen dollars a month to pasture a cow and her calf. A government lease costs only a few dollars, but there is no way for a person like me to get such a lease. The grazing permits are not granted to the highest bidder as they are in nearly every other sector of government. Instead, they are doled out in a seniority system that makes it virtually impossible for a permittee to lose his permit. When you consider that these public lands are also intended to be used for recreation and wildlife, the policy seems preposterous because the system encourages destruction of range through overgrazing, which limits wildlife habitat and recreational opportunities.

A very small percentage of the meat produced in the United States comes from public land, but every pound that is produced and dumped on the market hurts the price that private producers are paid for their product. If these private producers are not allowed to bid for these permits, they would be better off if grazing on public lands was disallowed altogether. Only the subsidized ranch operators who have control of these leases would suffer. There are very few of these people, but they have come to view the leases as their property. They even sell the leases along with the property they are attached to, sometimes for fabulous prices. Although most lease holders prefer not to admit it, the law grants the public the right of access on these lands.

The land around our campsite was public and usually good for sage grouse. Erney and I were anxious to give Spud a try. Because we didn't want to leave Dolly alone, we decided to take turns hunting with Spud and Jake. While one of us hunted, the other would stay in camp, cooking and keeping an eye peeled for anything that might harm Dolly.

I had heard about Spud from Bill Heinrich, the old friend who is my boss during the reintroduction season. Bill knew about a litter of English setters near Boise, Idaho. He was going to take a female and called to ask if I would be interested in a male. My only dog at the time was Jake, an old Labrador who really belonged to Kris, so I said sure. Both Spud's parents were champions; as a puppy he was known as Potato Head. Never has there been a dog more interested in birds and people. From the beginning, he was either trying to sit in your lap or chasing birds. At the ranch as a puppy he would chase the homing pigeons all day long. The pigeons were safe and they knew it, but to watch Spud chasing them made you think he was on the verge of his first kill. As far as I know, he never got within twenty feet of a pigeon, but his enthusiasm never waned.

There are different schools of thought on training pointing dogs. I have always believed that the most important quality is an interest in birds. If a dog is well bred, he will begin to point when he figures out that chasing birds gets him nowhere. Eventually the dog stops chasing and starts pointing without requiring the trainer to exercise pressure that could kill the dog's interest in birds altogether. But Spud liked to chase birds more than any dog I had ever seen, and I often wondered if he would ever stop.

Most dogs have poor eyesight, but Spud could see better than a person. One day, in the early spring before Spud was a year old, he and I were out in the yard when he suddenly perked up and stared intently at the horizon. He watched the sky for a few seconds, then ran as fast as he could toward the south. It was impossible to stop him, so I watched. He was nearly a half mile away when the stopped and looked straight up. I had no idea what he saw until I heard the plaintive sound of migrating sandhill cranes. The cranes were very high, and I did not see them until they were nearly over the house. Spud was right behind them, though several thousand feet below, running back and forth as he looked up. The cranes continued to migrate northward in their spiral and glide pattern and Spud stayed right under them. The cranes couldn't have known he was there. They were on their way to Canada and probably wouldn't stop until they got there. The last I saw of Spud that day was his tail disappearing over the ridge nearly a mile north of the house.

Erney let me hunt first. I started off through the sagebrush hoping that Spud would be as interested in sage grouse as he was in pigeons and cranes. Old Jake came along to flush any birds that Spud missed and to retrieve any that were shot. We must have looked like quite a team, me already soaked to the knees from the wet sage, Spud running far ahead at great speed, and Jake, veteran of many hunts, walking obediently at heel. I carried the shotgun that my father had left to me, a side-by-side twenty gauge.

The land rolled in long flat valleys, topped by ridges. The sagebrush and grass seemed too homogeneous to support game birds. But sage grouse are different from most game birds in several ways. One of the differences is that they find almost everything they need to survive in one plant. Not only do sage grouse prefer the sweet-smelling gray-green sagebrush, but they also need it. If sagebrush is destroyed so are the sage grouse. Their range is defined by the range of sagebrush. So close is the sage grouse associated with sagebrush that one begins to wonder if they might not be the same substance in different form.

Though sage grouse love sagebrush, man hates it. Over half the sagebrush present on the North American continent before Europeans came here is now gone. It has been grubbed out, plowed under, poisoned, and burned. Because farmers had never seen sagebrush and couldn't grasp that it was a necessary part of this new environment, they destroyed it. Sage grouse, like most wild animals, are highly resistant to the long-term effects of draught, floods, hunting pressure, freak storms, and natural predation, but they cannot withstand habitat destruction. This is the simplest of ecological facts, yet it is one of the least understood. Some people never seem to understand that increased demand for artichokes and asparagus destroys more wildlife than all the hunters combined.

But this was not the time to think about those things. Instead I turned my attention to Spud. He was the happiest dog on earth. He didn't have any idea what I was doing and, though he had been trained not to mind the noise, he had no idea why I was carrying the shotgun. He did know that he was supposed to remain in my sight and not chase rabbits, but he hadn't figured out that I would like him to stop, raise his tail high, and perhaps even raise a front paw when he smelled a sage grouse. He didn't even know what a sage grouse was.

The sagebrush in that part of Montana was only eighteen inches high so I could see Spud clearly a hundred yards ahead. Back and forth he went, fifty yards to the left, then fifty to the right. He ran like a greyhound and I watched to see if he was using his nose at all. Once I thought I saw him raise his head into the wind and start in that direction, but I wasn't sure; it could have been just wishful thinking. Jake plodded along beside me, his head high, searching the breeze for what he knew was out there. But he was a retriever, not a pointer; his main interest was in dead birds that he wanted to bring back to me. I have never figured out why retrievers bring things back and give them up. But that is what they live for. And pointing dogs live to find live birds. They will run all day without finding so much as a feather. All of it, the retrieving for what seemed no reward and the fruitless searching, seemed strange to me until I considered how I must look, surrounded by hundreds of square miles of sagebrush, walking up and down, one ridge after the other; walking with no apparent direction in mind.

I had been walking for an hour when I stopped to call Spud in for a rest. I wanted to pet him and let him know that I thought he was doing well, even though we had not seen any grouse. When I stopped, Jake lay down, sensibly conserving his energy in case we came across a field of dead birds in need of retrieving. Spud was still running. He had circled downwind and when I whistled he changed his direction and streaked straight for us. I bent over, encouraging him to come in, and he ran hard. So hard, in fact, that he nearly ran over a grouse before it got up and flew.

Jake and I both perked up. The big bird labored into the air and lined out for the top of the ridge. Spud, after getting himself under control, had miraculously stopped, as if he knew he should have pointed the grouse and flushing it had been an honest mistake. He stood tall, his tail solid over his back, his head high and his eyes bright. He watched the disappearing bird, looked back at me, back to the bird, then off he went, running faster than I had ever seen him run. That is when he ran into the whole flock of grouse. Six big males lifted in front of him and he altered his course to follow them. Then another group got up to his right and he went with them. In a moment the entire hillside got up and began to fly away. We had found the mother lode: A couple of hundred sage grouse pounded into the air. Because Spud hadn't pointed, I didn't shoot. I stood and watched my bird dog. He never slowed down. He wanted to catch them all.

I thought briefly about trying to call him in, but the grouse were making too much noise and besides, there was no chance he would respond. Jake, who had been excited at the possibility of a grouse dying so that he could bring it to me, sat down. He watched Spud charging here and there, leaping into the air, doubling back. Finally Spud disappeared over the hill behind a flock of twenty grouse. When Spud and all the grouse were gone, Jake looked up at me. He exhaled loudly and lay back down to wait.

We waited almost an hour. Twice Spud came

back, only to bump another grouse and take off after it. Finally, foot sore, tongue nearly dragging, and tail bloody from too much wagging in the sagebrush, he came in and lay down beside Jake. Jake got up and moved to a different spot. I looked down at Spud. It was not as discouraging as it seemed. Spud had proved again that he had the one thing that you can't teach a dog. He had heart, he was a hunter. It would have been ten times worse to see him disinterested in grouse. I bent down and stroked his head. From the corner of my eye, I saw Jake watching this. He looked away as if totally disgusted. I heard him exhale again, this time overly loud.

No one ate grouse that night. Erney was Spud's greatest supporter and said over and over that what had happened wasn't "too bad for a puppy's first day." He petted Spud's exhausted head. And later, as I returned with a load of firewood, I caught Spud curled up in Erney's lap as he sat reading by the light from the lantern.

Each day, for the next three, Dolly flew farther to the lure. Finally, she was coming a hundred feet, and the creance had begun to hinder her by catching on blades of grass. On the fifth day, Dolly flew free. It was the first time she had been free since her brothers and sister had been killed by the eagle.

Early that morning, I had blocked her and given her a bath. As we cooked and ate our breakfast, Dolly immersed herself in the water in the bath pan. She shook and dipped her feathers, submerged her head, shimmied down into the water as if she were settling on eggs. Erney and I watched her and knew that she was feeling at home. Her calmness made me even more sure that she was ready to fly free. So just before noon, after she had dried in the sun and preened her feathers, I picked her up on my fist and hooded her. Everything was exactly as it had been for the last four days, except that today I attached a tiny radio transmitter to her leg instead of the creance.

The dogs were put into the truck, not because Dolly was afraid of them but because on a first flight, even more than subsequent flights, Murphy's Law is in effect.

Erney brought the radio receiver out and checked to be sure the transmitter was working, then he leaned against the hood of the pickup, ready if I needed help. The last two days, Dolly had left the perch before I took the lure out of my hawking bag. This was a good sign. It meant she was actually being called out of the air to the lure, exactly what she would be expected to do in the very near future. There were several stages in the process of teaching her about the lure. The first was simply to come from the perch to the lure; the second was to come to the lure after she was flying. The third was, once in the air, to change direction and come. And the final stage was to stop her from chasing something and make her come back to the lure. Already we had achieved the first two. Today I would let her fly past me and try to call her back. It was not impossible that she would keep going, right past me, gaining altitude, faster and faster, until finally she would simply disappear. Imagining this moments before a falcon's first flight leads you to look for any excuse to postpone the flight: The wind is too strong, you think, or the sun too bright, or the falcon not hungry enough. I considered all the possible reasons for calling off that first flight, yet I knew, as I walked out to put Dolly on her perch, that flying her free was the reason we were there. The rest of falconry was simply bird keeping. Peregrines fly free, I thought: Birds that sit for years on blocks or in cages were something else.

In the traditional way, with my right hand and my teeth, I loosened the braces holding the hood on Dolly's head, then lifted it off and clipped it onto the hawking bag. Then I put her on the perch and she was free. I walked away keeping an eye on her to see if she would fly before I called her. When I was only ten feet away she took off. It was as if she knew that nothing held her to earth. She made two hard elevating flaps and passed me at eye level. Suddenly I realized how my affection for her had grown, and was tempted to call her down with the lure immediately. Instead, I waited. She watched me as she went by, then looked straight ahead, pumping her wings deeply, testing things, remembering how it had felt to fly free in the mountains. I waited as long as I could, until she was twenty-five yards beyond me, then pulled the lure from the bag, and swung it around my head. I whistled sharply. Though she was still going away, she looked over her shoulder and pivoted in the air. I let the lure fall to the ground and she glided onto it before it stopped moving.

She fed on the lure as if nothing out of the ordinary had happened. The lure was concealed from my view by the short buffalo grass, and she looked exactly like a wild peregrine feeding on a fresh kill. The difference, of course, was that I was there, kneeling in the grass with her. She paid no attention to me, letting me reattach her jesses as if I were a creature of no significance whatever. When we walked back into camp, Erney was smiling. We didn't say much as Dolly finished her meal on my fist, but we both thought that it was time we found a few ponds with ducks on them. We both knew that Dolly would be ready in a few days, ready to start her migration, her real life.

❧

That afternoon, after Erney left with a shotgun and the two dogs, I scouted for ducks. The high plains are breeding grounds for hundreds of thousands of ducks. The remaining natural wetlands and the stock ponds that ranchers have created harbor resident families of mallard, teal, gadwall, pintail, widgeon, shoveler, redhead, lesser scaup, and even a few canvasbacks. When adults arrive in early spring, some are already paired up and begin to breed shortly after the ice has cleared. By early summer, the hens are sitting on eggs tucked neatly into the prairie grass, and the drakes gather on bachelor ponds. In the spring there are ducks on almost every pond. But by June a strange thing happens. Suddenly, the ducks disappear, or seem to disappear. Actually, they are still there, but they must depend on their ability to hide for protection. The ducks have molted their main feathers and have become flightless. They have lost their bright breeding plumage and are concentrating on surviving the summer. The drakes slip in and out of the water with barely a ripple and spend most of their time in the grass near the edge of the ponds. The hens are even more secretive because they are incubating eggs. When the ducklings hatch, their ability to remain unseen is their only protection.

It is not until September that you notice the ducks again. When the nights turn cool and autumn seems just around the corner, they appear in great numbers. It is about this time that the northern ducks are driven south by bad weather and the wetlands of the high plains serve as gathering sites for the migrations that are about to begin. So that first afternoon when I went looking for ducks, I found them. But this was a scouting trip and I was looking for certain kinds of ducks on certain kinds of ponds. I was looking for ducks that might be good first prey for Dolly.

Ducks are a natural prey of peregrine falcons. Though peregrines prefer smaller birds, they have always been associated with ducks. In fact, for many years they were called duck hawks. But not all ducks are the same. A teal weighs about twelve ounces (the size of a pigeon), while the largest ducks—canvasbacks, mallards, and mergansers—weigh about three pounds, a full pound more than Dolly. An unlucky tussle with a drake mallard could turn a peregrine falcon off. In the wild they would be more likely to try a small duck first and only later go after a mallard. In order to plan Dolly's first hunt successfully, I had to consider the size of the quarry, the amount of water involved, the wind direction and velocity, and the position of any obstacles that an overzealous young falcon might collide with.

I drove past several ponds with small groups of mallards. One pond had teal on it but a telephone wire, a danger to all falcons, stretched across the downwind end. I saw several ponds way off in the distance and walked out to study them with my binoculars. A small group of widgeons swam on a wet spot in a draw, but there were pintails mixed with them that Dolly might choose to chase. Nothing seemed quite right until I came to a low place where the road had been very wet and was now nearly impassable because of the deep, hard ruts. I was busy driving and almost didn't notice the water lingering south of the road. From the corner of my eye, I saw three teal. It was perfect. The only problem was that Dolly would not be ready for a few more days and there seemed a very good chance that the pond would dry up and the teal would leave.

I would just have to wait and see. I drove to camp the long way because I didn't want to double back and take the chance of frightening the teal. On the way, a herd of antelope ran madly alongside me. They wanted to cross the road, and for some reason they had determined that they could not wait until I passed. They raced to get ahead of me. Finally I stopped, refusing to be a party to such a ridiculous contest, and let them cross in front of me. I counted thirty-two of them, all does and kids. The very last one in line was an old dry doe. She had hurt her leg and was far behind. But still she ran, hustling as best she could. She would not make it through the coming winter, and it made me feel bad when she looked at me with panic in her eyes, as if I might rev up the engine of my pickup and run her down in cold blood.

The image of the old doe's face stuck with me all the way back to camp, but when I saw Erney leaning over our little table with a knife, I forgot about the antelope. He heard me and turned to look with a broad smile. Then, as I pulled the pickup to a stop, he held up the sage grouse he was cleaning. It was a big male, six pounds at least, and Erney held it proudly. He pointed at the grouse, then toward the ground. Again and again, with a big smile, he pointed to the grouse and then toward the ground. It was not until I got out of the pickup that I realized he was not pointing at the ground, but at Spud who lay at Erney's feet. Spud held his head high and looked regal and proud.

As it turned out, Spud had only held the point for a few seconds. But since our policy was to only shoot over points and it had, I was assured, been a point, Erney shot the grouse. That, according to Erney, is when a strange thing happened. Jake, who weighed ninety pounds, leaped forward. Finally, something dead to bring back. But, since Spud had been right behind the bird when it fell, he got there first. It was the first bird that Spud had ever gotten close to, and a big one. Erney said the grouse had fallen dead, and Spud, no doubt not fully understanding that the bird had been shot, figured that at last he had caught one. He lunged at the inanimate bird while running at top speed. The result was a terrible wreck, sagebrush and dust flying. Apparently the dog rolled twice, but when the dust cleared, forty-two-pound Spud came up with the six-pound bird in his mouth, face-to-face with ninety-pound Jake. Erney said it was the first time he had ever heard Spud growl. "Funniest sound I ever heard," Erney said. "Kind of high-pitched and distorted by all the dust and feathers."

It is probably a good thing that Erney was right there. Once Jake goes out to retrieve something, he doesn't like to come back with nothing. If Spud was determined to hold on to the grouse, Jake might have just brought the whole works back. But Erney was there, and after some cajoling, he talked Spud out of his grouse. "He quit hunting," Erney said. "Just followed me around and growled at old Jake every time he came near." I looked around and saw that Jake was sleeping a few yards away. He had forgotten about the whole thing. But Spud lay just under the table where the grouse was being cleaned. He was still alert, keeping watch. I knelt down to look at him, and I swear his eyes were deeper, his head more square, his neck a little stouter.

Perhaps it was the fresh air and exercise, but for days I had been thinking of food. After a few days in camp, we stopped listening to the radio. Foreign affairs were no longer an issue. It didn't matter. But food did. I had begun to crave the dark red meat of sage grouse, the dusty wild plums that grew in the draws with their bitter skins and sweet flesh, and I looked in a different way at the mule deer that grazed the sage flats. Erney had felt it too, and like our food-gathering ancestors, he had begun to collect the meadow mushrooms that grew in the prairie's few damp places.

That night we ate grouse—thick, medium-rare slices of breast meat. We smothered it in onions, fried potatoes, peppers, and the mushrooms we had found. We ate everything we had cooked, and still chewed on legs long after we were usually in bed. We watched the stars and I told Erney about the teal I had found. Neither of us said it, but I'm sure we both thought the same thing. With any luck we would be eating duck soon. The fresh meat had made us hungry for more.

We had begun to hunt. As José Ortega y Gasset says in *Meditations on Hunting,* we were now more than spectators of nature. We were part of it; physically and spiritually we were finding our way back. A Laguna woman once told me that hunting is not a matter of outwitting or overpowering animals. She laughed at the suggestion that a man could consistently kill animals that did not want to die. "Love them," she said. "Show them that you respect them and they will come and give themselves to you. It doesn't take much," she said. "A little ritual to honor them." The Laguna woman was a deer hunter. She almost never came home without her deer, so I took what she said very seriously.

The weather stayed nice, but the pond where I had found the teal did not dry up. Each day I encouraged Dolly to fly a little longer. Her strength and coordination increased. She began to catch the lure in the air, then to stoop at it repeatedly as I pulled it out of her reach. In the next few days she learned the bare essentials of flying and grasping moving objects at the same time. She was amazingly agile, what falconers call a good "footer," and soon it was not easy for me to keep the lure out of her grasp. When she could make ten hard stoops at the moving lure, I decided she was ready to try the teal.

It is important to get the falcon flying at game as soon as possible. They naturally prefer chasing birds to stooping at a lure, but they can become so used to the lure that they don't seem to recognize birds as game and may ignore them. It is natural at this early stage in a falcon's development for the falconer to dream about classic stoops at difficult quarry from tremendously high pitches. But what is more important for a young falcon is success, which builds confidence. If the falcon meets with early success at easy quarry and the difficulty of the flights is gradually increased, the dramatic flights will come. But you must take one step at a time.

※

The day of Dolly's first slip—her first chance to catch game—began with a vivid sunrise. The eastern sky was streaked with pink and gold, the horizon ribbed with low stratus clouds. The sunrise was the result of a front that had moved down in the night. It was cold and there was ice on Dolly's bath pan. We had been at that camp for ten days and had felt the gradual change in the weather. Though it had rained when we first arrived, it had not been cold. We had a week of Indian summer, but now there was a bite to the morning air. It was the second week in October. We had shot and eaten several grouse and Dolly had been switched from her diet of domestic quail to parts of the wild grouse. The combination of the nutritious food and the cool air made her keen. She looked ready.

Before we left, we fixed the transmitter to Dolly's leg as usual. I prepared the lure and Erney tied the dogs to make sure they wouldn't try to follow us.

The same band of antelope that I had seen ran parallel to us. This time they were on the other side of the road, but still they were not happy and crossed back to the side where I had originally seen them. We stopped as they strung out in front of us. The crippled doe was still with them, a little farther behind perhaps, and again she seemed terrified as she ran in front of the pickup. Erney agreed that she would not make it through the winter and this sudden thought of mortality sobered me. All through the morning a cloud bank had been building in the north. It looked like snow.

I let the pickup roll to a halt at the top of the hill, just before the road started down to the low spot where I had seen the teal. I fixed a spotting scope to the window on the driver's side. At first the little pond seemed empty, and I was disappointed. But just as I was about to give up, a duck swam out from the bank. It was a teal, and in a minute it was joined by the other two. The situation was just as I had hoped it would be, three teal on a very small pond. Our plan was to let Dolly loose about fifty yards from the pond. She would circle around, waiting for me to produce the lure, while we crept up to the pond, hidden behind the dike. As long as ducks stay on the water they are safe from falcons. Falcons like to take their quarry from the air. We would wait until Dolly was flying toward us, still looking for the lure, and then we would raise up and flush the teal in front of her.

After parking the pickup, I strapped the hawking bag to my waist and picked Dolly up on my fist. We circled far around to be sure that the teal would not see us. Then, hidden behind the dike, we moved closer to the pond. The ground at the bottom of the draw was soft and our boots were muddy by the time we reached the place where Dolly would be launched. Erney and I looked at each other. Erney shrugged. "Here we go," he said.

When I eased the hood off, Dolly looked at the cloud bank to the north as if she knew exactly what it meant. She stared at it for several seconds through half-closed eyes, then roused, shaking her whole body violently. When she finished the rouse, her feathers were slicked down and her eyes were full and round. She spread her wings and, still clutching my fist, beat them three times very hard. Then I felt her ease her grip. When she beat her wings again she became airborne, pumping with purpose into the cool wind that seemed to come from the gathering clouds.

She flew into the wind for thirty yards, then turned and soared over us, looking for the lure. I made no move to reach into the hawking bag. Keeping our eyes on her, Erney and I walked steadily toward the pond. She came back over, again looking for the lure, then veered off and flew directly over the pond. I could hear the teal whistling to each other as she came into sight. She looked down at them from a height of only forty feet, then headed back toward us. By then, we were nearly to the dike. She flew back into the wind and turned to make a pass at us. As she was flying downwind, we stood up, waving our hands at the teal. They sprang from the water just as Dolly passed overhead. They were right in her path.

It was not the thousand-foot vertical stoop that one strives for, and the quarry did not fly sure and strong the way a sharp-tailed grouse might, but it worked. When the teal flushed, Dolly altered her course and tried to catch the last one in line. She did not hit it hard, but the teal fell on the bare dirt at the edge of the pond, very much like a lure tossed on the ground for her. She pitched up neatly and settled on the teal before it regained its balance and ran back to the water. She looked only slightly surprised when the teal struggled. In a matter of seconds, she reached down with her beak and severed the teal's neck vertebrae as if she had done it many times before.

Erney and I stood close by, letting her enjoy her kill, wanting her to be encouraged by what she had done. "Funny it didn't make it back to the water," Erney said. I agreed. There had been something too easy about the way Dolly had held the teal once they were on the ground.

We both sat close to her while she fed. She held the teal breast-down by both wings and pulled feathers from its back. The feathers floated with the cooling breeze until a wedge of them covered the earth. She plucked feathers merrily until she came to the scant meat on the teal's bony back. She stripped and ate the meat, clearly enjoying its warmth and freshness. Then she rolled the teal on its back and began to pluck its breast. That is when Erney noticed the broken leg of the teal. "No wonder he was so slow on his feet," he said. I nodded and looked away from the teal toward the clouds to the north. "He wouldn't have made it through winter, either," Erney said.

As soon as I got the chance, I reached slowly over and removed the duck's head. I continued to watch Dolly eat, but dug a hole in the mud beside me and inserted the head, covering it and smoothing the earth with my bare hand.

That night we got our first snow. The temperature had continued to drop all that day, and by sunset it was well below freezing. The snow started as an almost imperceptible patter against the canvas tent. As I lay in the dark going over what had happened that day, I thought the gentle drumming of the snow was the sound of moth's wings. That night it seemed possible that moths, perhaps all the moths in the world, were trying to get into the tent.

The next morning, when I stuck my head outside, the world was white. I closed the tent flap, and as I knelt, shivering in my underwear, to re-stoke the fire, I thought I heard another sound. This sound was more familiar but still, in the new white morning, eerie and unreal. Erney heard it too and turned his head in the sleeping bag to listen. The sound came from the dam behind the tent. In the night, through the first snow of winter, the geese had come.

All that morning, while we made breakfast and packed the camp, they honked their melancholy song of migration. We kept the dogs from going up to the dam and chasing them away. It sounded like there were hundreds of them on the water just out of our sight. We did not want to disturb them, but once the camp had been loaded into the pickup, we sneaked to the top of the dam to look.

They were Canadas, the first we'd seen come down, a sign that lakes were freezing farther north. They swam in the pond, stood on the snowy bank, and flew short distances along the shore. We watched them, hidden behind some willows, for twenty minutes. We wondered where they had begun their migration, where they would go, and how they knew the way. But we didn't watch and wonder for long. It was cold there in the snow and we had our own migration to think of.

We drove a hundred miles south, back across the upper Missouri and noticed that the cottonwoods' brilliant gold was complete. In another day some of the leaves would begin to fall. They would float on the surface of the Missouri like tiny bullboats racing to reach St. Louis before the water froze. We drove into the Judith Basin and then into the Musselshell drainage. We wandered for three days before we set our camp up on the land of Merle and Gladys Busenbark.

We put Dolly out to weather while we pitched the tent. After camp was made and Dolly had bathed and preened, we drove over to see the Busenbarks and Kent Carnie. Kent, a retired army colonel, parked his motor home on Merle's land for several weeks each autumn. It was one of his stops as he moved southward much as we were doing. He wasn't in his trailer, but we found him sitting at the Busenbarks' kitchen table eating hot cinnamon rolls as fast as Gladys could haul them from the oven.

Kent and Merle were good friends, though very different. Kent was originally from California, had been educated at Berkeley and Princeton, and had traveled all over the world connected with military intelligence. Although Kent's main interest was falconry and the history of the sport, he was extremely well read, kept his radio tuned to the closest public radio station and, if asked, could name almost any piece of classical music that was played. Merle, on the other hand, had spent almost his entire life in the middle of Montana. The ranch had belonged to his father before him and it was many miles over gravel roads to a town with a post office. Merle, in many ways, was a very simple man. He was formally uneducated and lived frugally. But for all his provincial ways, Merle had been mentioned in several national magazines, including *Time*.

In most sections of America, quick-money farm practices are initiated at the expense of sound, long-range, management principles. Usually the long-range effects are ignored. But Merle and a few of his neighbors refused to ignore the practice of plowing up native grass so that the landowner, in this case a businessman from town, could plant wheat that would qualify him for larger loans at the bank. Wheat does not grow well in Merle's county and you can't make farmland out of grassland simply by plowing it. Merle had lived there all his life and knew that the soil simply washed and blew away once the natural cover was plowed under. As the erosion fouled everything, the guilty parties would take their profits and move on, leaving people like Merle to deal with the aftermath. Merle fought a large corporate project planned for his county and won. The result was that restrictions were placed on the plowing of native grass in that county. To this day it is one of only two counties in the country with such restrictions.

Kent and Merle talked about land while I ate my cinnamon roll and listened. The table was crooked because one side of the tiny room was lower than the other. The house was small and in need of paint, and I imagined it as cold and drafty in the Montana winter. Merle talked about the cows that he wanted to round up in a few days to vaccinate. The calves they produced each year were his only cash crop, his entire income. Even in the best years, Merle and his family would be considered among the nation's poor. There must have been a moment during Merle's fight against the plowing of native grass when it occurred to him that he could just keep his mouth shut, plow up his own land, and make more money than he would make with his little cowherd in twenty years. But of course, that was not something Merle would do. He extracted a promise from Kent to help with the roundup, then looked at his watch. "Time to fly the falcons," he said and everyone at the table smiled.

Raised in captivity, Kent's falcon is a peregrine-gyrfalcon hybrid, and veteran of many seasons of sharptailed grouse hunting. Grouse are a classic quarry of the large falcons, the maximum test of a falcon's skill. If grouse were much harder to catch they would be impossible. There are probably only a few trained falcons who have killed more than Kent's falcon, Blue Bell, who was named after the fragile light blue prairie flower found over most of the northern plains. But Blue Bell is anything but fragile. She is a big, dark, powerful falcon, capable of stooping hard enough to kill a grouse instantly.

Merle asked if I wanted to fly Dolly at sharp-tails, and I declined, explaining that she was not ready for grouse. He nodded, and promised a grouse slip for Kent and a duck for us. Merle was something of a falcon connoisseur and took pride in guiding us. He had seen lots of falcons fly and knew them. He also knew his land. There was a group of grouse on the edge of a pasture not far from a pond where he had seen a few mallards the day before.

Kent's dog was a Brittany spaniel named Muffin who was nearly too old to do much hunting. Because of Muffin's age I was tempted to volunteer Spud's services. Luckily I remained quiet. Though he had been doing well, it was not realistic for me to think that Spud could perform with the discipline needed to work with a hunting falcon. I leaned against the pickup, watching Muffin cast out toward the pasture corner at a wise, geriatric gait. The wind was in our faces, and Muffin raised her head as she quartered into it. Kent had been hunting with falcons for almost forty years. He had sensed the presence of game thousands of times, but still his excitement was fresh and immediate.

When Muffin raised her head, Kent became animated. The old dog moved in closer and bumped a grouse. Everyone groaned, but Merle was not discouraged. "There's more," he said. "At least a dozen in this corner." One of the worst things a falconer can do is put his falcon up over nothing. Falcons need to know that there will always be quarry if they go up over the falconer and wait-on. Kent looked at Merle then back at Muffin. The dog was still birdy, so Kent decided to take a chance. Before he took Blue Bell's hood off, he made sure that Muffin would not move prematurely by projecting his best military "Whoa." The way he said that word would put the brakes on a salty drill sergeant. Muffin didn't move a muscle.

Blue Bell left his fist and made a low circle before gaining altitude. She, too, was just beginning for the season, and her movements were slightly stiff. But she knew the game and soon was up two hundred feet. Kent mumbled to himself as we waited for her to gain more altitude and get into position. Muffin trembled with excitement.

When Blue Bell was as high as she would go, Kent moved ahead. He stopped beside the dog and looked over his shoulder toward Blue Bell. As she moved forward, slightly upwind of where the grouse should be, Kent turned and started in. He sent Muffin ahead. She scurried back and forth like a rat terrier. They combed the grass ahead of them, but no grouse came up. It was too late to start over, and I could feel Kent's frustration at not being able to produce a grouse for Blue Bell. Merle, standing three feet from me, said calmly, "They're there, keep going." He said it too softly for Kent to hear, but just then Muffin put them up.

I watched the grouse, and had counted eleven of them by the time Blue Bell's stoop flattened out and she overtook the last one. Apparently, she was slightly out of position when the grouse flushed, and she was not going fast enough to hit hard. Even so, she bound to the last grouse, pulled it in, and set her wings to take it to the ground.

When we got to her, Blue Bell had neatly broken the grouse's neck and stood on top of it, plucking feathers delicately. Muffin sat happily nearby, salivating slightly, waiting for her share. Soon Kent would move slowly toward Blue Bell and convince her to leave the grouse for his fist. He was delighted and beamed with pride.

We left him like that and headed toward the pond where Merle had seen the mallards. By this time Dolly had caught several ducks and could handle mallards. Because I intended to set her free when we reached southern Texas, I wanted her to have the kind of experiences that a wild falcon would have. I intended to fly her in ways that most trained falcons were not flown. Gradually, I wanted to become less a part of her hunting. The truth is that falconers protect their birds from the grim realities of natural selection. For Dolly to have any chance after I was gone, I would have to hold my protective impulses to a minimum. I would have to wean Dolly and myself at the same time.

There were six mallards on a pond the size of a football field. The more water ducks have, the greater the chance they will flush when the falcon is in poor position, and escape with ease. It takes a smart falcon, flying very high, to catch ducks off big water. Although this pond was not huge, it would provide Dolly's most challenging flight to date. Still half a mile away, we looked the pond over with binoculars. It was late afternoon and the wind was light; even so, I was sure we would have some trouble getting the mallards to leave the pond at the right time. Finally we decided on a plan. Erney and Merle would approach the pond from the upstream side so that they could keep the mallards from landing again once they were flushed. Jake and I would approach from the downstream side, using the dam to hide us. We would do the initial flushing.

When I opened the back of the pickup, Jake leapt out before getting the signal. This was his favorite sport. He knew exactly what was going on. He jumped and pranced like a puppy in front of Spud who had been made to stay in the pickup. As soon as we started walking, Spud began to howl. It started sharply, almost like barking, but deteriorated into pitiful, high-pitched notes that lingered for what seemed like minutes before they faded and began again. Spud was clearly feeling bad about being left behind, but Jake, walking at heel as if he were restrained by an invisible leash, seemed pleased with the situation. He strained against the invisible leash, panted as if his collar encumbered his breathing, and smiled a long-tongued, slobbery smile each time Spud's howls reached maximum pitch.

It seemed likely that the mallards would flush, draw Dolly down in a stoop, land back on the water, wait until she was too low to catch them, then flush for good. I wanted to flush them well the first time so I made Jake sit just below the dam on one end and I went to the other end. That way we could both come over the top at the same time and have a better chance of getting the mallards to fly. This was the hardest part for Jake. I had told him in a whisper to "sit" and punctuated "stay" with a firm index finger across the muzzle. He panted with nerves and trembled as I walked to my position. He watched as I took the hood off Dolly and stood up when she flew. I held up my hand, scowled, and moved a few steps in his direction. He sat back down, watched Dolly gaining altitude and trembled even more.

Her wing beats had become much stronger in the last week. They were no longer deep and slow; now they were shallow and crisp. Her increased speed was deceptive. The strength in the wings allowed her to cover distances much more quickly than it appeared. In the days since her first kill she had begun to mount to a pitch of several hundred feet and wait there until she saw a chance. That evening she went higher than she had ever gone before. We waited until she was right overhead, then I waved Jake over the top of the bank.

The mallards left the water just as ninety pounds of dog entered it. They flew as we thought they would fly, over the water, waiting for the falcon to stoop so that they could put back into the pond safely. Dolly was not yet crafty enough to wait until they had committed themselves before she started her stoop. She rolled on the mallards and they would have put down and gotten away, if Erney and Merle hadn't stood up at the other end of the pond.

We had planned well: The mallards kept going, out over the prairie, and gave Dolly a shot. She folded her wings and fell like a stone. The mallard she chose was a drake, an easy target for a wild peregrine. But Dolly did not hit him with all the force of her stoop. In fact, she did not hit him at all. She pulled up when he rolled to avoid her. Then she pitched up, expecting him to give up so she could flutter down on him when he landed. But the drake did not surrender. Once the force of her stoop was spent, and she pitched up like a true rookie, the drake exploded with a kind of speed Dolly had never seen before. He flew at a forty-five-degree angle, away and gone, and it was Dolly who quit.

Clearly she was surprised at the way the drake mallard had acted. She was also surprised to find there was nothing on the lure except a few feathers and one bite of duck. She pulled at the lure in disbelief. Her disbelief turned to anger and finally, just before I slipped the hood on her head, her feathers went slick and her eyes darkened with the realization that dinner had flown away from her. It was a lesson, clumsily taught, but one that was part of her reality. When I turned from hooding her, the Montana sun was going down. Merle smiled and shook his head. "That's the way it goes," he said. "Out here, if you want to eat, you better catch something." He was absolutely right. It was the primary law of survival. But as we made our way back to the pickup, I was plagued by a nagging sensation that it was all an arrogant construct. Who was I to enforce a law with such primordial implications?

The
GRASSLANDS

T he nights turned cold. One morning, I found a half inch of ice in Dolly's bath pan. It was time to leave Montana. But there was one more stop we wanted to make before we pointed the pickup toward the Gulf of Mexico.

In the town of Winifred, Montana, lived old friends whom I had met eighteen years before. Ralph Rodgers and his wife, Missy, had moved from West Texas to Winifred because they were convinced they would have a better life there. They felt their children would have a better childhood and grow up to be the kind of people Ralph and Missy wanted them to be if they were raised with access to Montana's mountains and plains. I have heard this sentiment from many people, but the Rodgerses are about the only ones who actually did anything about it. Ralph had studied biology and had a choice between becoming a science teacher or going on for an advanced degree studying sea otters. They had agonized over the decision but finally figured that teaching would be best for their kids, Scott and Andi. A few years after I met them, hunting pheasants on the wheat flats of eastern Colorado, they found jobs in a tiny, remote school district in central Montana and have been there ever since.

The occasion for our visit, beyond friendship, was Scott Rodgers's last high school football game. In small towns like Winifred, they play football differently from the rest of America. They play it with six men on a side. I had played a little football, both in high school and college, but I had never seen a six-man game. I had been told that it was a very different game. Ralph, a critic of high school athletics when in competition with academics, was also a proud father and supporter of the community. He had been after me for years to attend a game, and when I had talked with him earlier in the fall, he had said that this was my last chance; Scott would be graduating.

We arrived just after noon and found the high school and the football field without asking directions. It turned out that the Rodgerses' house was across the street from the school. Because there were no lights for night games, the game was to start at two-thirty. By one o'clock when we pulled up behind the bleachers, there were already a dozen people milling around. There was a chill in the air and, to the northwest, a gray cloud bank threatened snow. But above the football field at Winifred, Montana, the sky was clear blue and the sun shone brightly. A perfect day for football.

There is no lock on the door of the Rodgerses' house, and kids come and go all day as if the little house were an annex to the school. Ralph's falcon was blocked out at one end of his covered weathering yard, and I blocked Dolly at the other end. Erney and I were standing in the yard looking over the fence to the football field when Ralph emerged from the front door with part of a sandwich in his hand and a mouth full of ham and cheese. "You made it," he said through the ham and cheese.

"Yeah. Thought you'd be teaching."

"I come home for lunch," Ralph said. "You want a sandwich?"

Erney and I nodded and followed Ralph into the house. We sliced thick pieces of ham and cheddar while Ralph talked. "Missy is getting the pep band ready. She's the music department. The kids should be getting out right after lunch." Ralph looked at his watch. "Any time now. The game starts in an hour and a half. Big game," he said. "We play Roy." I had to think for a minute. Roy, yes, that was the sign we had seen at the road junction thirty miles from Winifred. I remembered a gas station, but that was all.

Ralph took three cans of lemonade from the refrigerator and after handing one to Erney and one to me, sat down at the table. He told us that Missy was overworked, that Andi, their daughter, was the star of junior high school and that Scott was applying to the military academies. He complained a little about the Board of Education, then told us that after the game he planned to cook a salmon that Scott had brought back from his summer fishing job in Alaska. He showed us the fish, a ten-pounder at least. Then he showed us the lemons and the almonds he planned to cook with it.

When we walked over to the game, Missy was slashing the air with a baton in front of six or eight kids of mixed ages blowing an assortment of brass instruments. She hailed us with her deep voice and Texas accent. When she turned to talk, the baton stopped, and the music began to trail off. It was as if the movement of the baton put air through the horns. She turned back to the band and cracked the baton crisply a few times. The music regained its tempo and she looked over her shoulder at us. "I'll talk to you later," she said.

The bleachers, capacity forty, were full. Thin men wearing cowboy hats and boots gathered along the sidelines. A half dozen kids sat on top of the school bus and three dogs chased each other around one of the end zones. On the field the teams were warming up. It seemed very much like any other high school football game unless you looked closely. First, there were not enough people, either in the stands or on the field. Twelve ragged jerseys marked Winifred ran back and forth at one end of the field. At the other end of the field, there were thirteen jerseys marked Roy. Even though the field was not the full one hundred yards, there still seemed to be a lot of space between players.

"It's a wide-open game," Ralph said as we took our place along the sideline with the stubbly cheeked ranchers. "You have to pass once before you run," Ralph said. He thought for a moment. He held his camera with its huge lens cradled in his arms and looked at the ground in deep thought. Then he turned to a man dressed in the greasy clothes of a mechanic. "Johnny," Ralph said, "do you have to pass before you run or after?"

The man shook his head. "Can't be after. Must be before, but laterals count."

"No," a cowboy-hatted man said. "Only forward

passes count for that rule. The main thing is that the ball has to touch two different players every play."

"Sure," a heavy lady said, "but only after the ball has traveled twenty yards."

Ralph led us away. "Anyway, it's a wide-open game," he said.

Because the grade school and the high school are in the same building, the bleachers and sidelines swarmed with young children. They ran up and down, playing tag, being caught here and there by women with handkerchiefs and eyes for runny noses. (It didn't seem to matter if the woman was the mother or not.) The children squealed and chased each other in hand-me-down blue jeans. Children lunged into one set of adult arms after another.

But when the game began, everyone's attention turned to the field. It was very different from what I had grown up with. Not only did everyone know the players on *their* team, but they also knew the players on the *other* team. The parents mixed on the sidelines, and a good play was cheered by everyone. What was amazing to me was how they knew which plays were good.

Ralph had been right. It was a wide-open game. Basically the ball was hiked and everyone went out for a pass. Sometimes a halfback would stay close to the quarterback and they would lateral the ball back and forth a couple of times before one of them would release a "Hail Mary" pass. There were plays that I had only heard about; the Statue of Liberty, flea flickers, double cross-buck laterals. Everyone ran and everyone handled the ball. Scott Rodgers was the center, but that didn't stop him from catching passes. There was no platoon system; almost everybody played both ways. Occasionally the referee would call a penalty for things like insufficient number of laterals or not enough people downfield. Twice both coaches were called to the middle of the field to explain their understanding of the rules. Once the mechanic was called out to give his opinion. And near the end of the fourth quarter Ralph walked out on the field right in among the players and took a picture of Scott just as he hiked the ball. He had to hustle off because, seeing an opportunity for a screen, one of the Winifred players button-hooked right in front of him. Nobody said anything.

The score was sixty-two to forty-seven. Winifred lost, but nobody seemed upset. As we waited for the salmon to finish cooking, Scott seemed to be happy that it was over. Getting beaten didn't depress him. Instead of brooding over the game the way I had at his age, he began to talk about his summer in Alaska. Here was a boy of seventeen who had found a job on a fishing boat, a hard job usually done by hard men. I had worked in Alaska myself and had some idea of the things that went on with the men who worked the boats. It must have been quite a shock for Scott, but he seemed to have thrived on it. If he got into one of the military academies, I thought, it would be the academy that was lucky.

It was a lovely evening. The clouds that had hung in the northwest made for a nice sunset, and we sat in the yard talking and drinking beer while we waited for the fish. Andi and Jake had become immediate friends, and the two of them played fetch with a stick for hours in the front yard. At one point Erney, Ralph, and I fell silent for several minutes just watching them. Andi was

a happy girl and showed no signs of the false sophistica-
tion of many girls her age. With all the joy in the world,
she threw the stick for Jake who charged after it and
brought it back with equal joy. She would kneel in the
grass, a beautiful young girl not as big as the dog, and
thank him for bringing back the stick. She put her arms
around his neck and hugged him, talked to him as if
he could understand. And as we watched them, I became sure that he could. I could see that Andi's faith
made it so.

We ate the salmon, and drank more beer until
Andi and Scott went to bed. Before Erney and I rolled
our sleeping bags out on the floor, we sat around the
kitchen table with Ralph and Missy and listened while
they talked about their life. Scott would be gone soon,
Andi only a few years later. What would they do? They
didn't know. In a way they had reached their goal.
Missy smiled and laughed. "We'll think of something,"
she said. Then she looked at Ralph. "Maybe we'll go
back to school. Ralph always wanted a Ph.D." Ralph
looked embarrassed. But the embarrassment turned
wistful.

"I had a chance," he said. "Sea otters. Had a
chance to study sea otters."

Missy reached out and put her hand on his arm.
"We'll see," she said. "Maybe those old sea otters could
still use you." He nodded and they looked at each other
in a way that made me envy them.

The cloud bank chased us southward. We
stopped near a pond in the sagebrush north of Billings,

and Dolly caught a gadwall out of a flock of twenty. While she fed on the duck, Erney took Spud and a shotgun for a walk and killed a sage grouse. He also found more meadow mushrooms. We stashed the grouse, mushrooms, and what was left of the duck behind the seat of the pickup and headed east, toward my South Dakota ranch, just as the first flakes of snow hit the windshield.

Before we reached the South Dakota border, the snow was coming hard and the wind had picked up. The drifts became steadily worse, and my pickup slid and spun until we could go no farther. The interstate was closed. We had to spend the night in Sundance, Wyoming. I had been stopped by snow once before in Sundance. As Erney's cold fingers fumbled with the motel keys and I stood behind him with our bags, the memory of that day chilled me more deeply than the blizzard whirling around my head.

I had been working for the Peregrine Fund out of Fort Collins, Colorado, for a couple of months, and when I was finished, I was anxious to get back home to South Dakota. My transportation was my old single-engine Cessna 170 and, even though the weather in Fort Collins was good, the Federal Flight Service told me that there was a snowstorm centered around the Black Hills and that it would be hard to reach the ranch. I waited for two days, basking in glorious Colorado sunshine and finding it steadily more difficult to believe there was really a storm in the Dakotas. Finally, of course, I tried it.

The blue sky held all the way past Cheyenne,

Torrington, and Lusk. But a cloud bank hung north of Newcastle, just as the flight service had said. I should have stopped in Newcastle, hitched a ride into town, had a meal and a few beers, and gone to bed. Twelve hours later, a day at the most, the snow would have moved east and I could have flown over the Black Hills and landed at my ranch without taking any chances. But as I approached Newcastle, I saw a light spot in the cloud bank to the northwest, and it occurred to me that I could follow the highway and see if that light spot was maybe a way through.

I'd been flying about 7,500 feet and had to come down quickly to slide under the clouds that hung over the road to Moorcroft. There were snow showers here and there, but every time I thought that I'd gone as far as I dared, an opening would reveal itself and, like Spud falling for a mother bird's broken wing routine, I went for it. By the time I reached Moorcroft and found Interstate 90 heading for Sundance and home, I was encountering clouds that spread all the way to the ground. Occasionally, I had to fly through them and they would splat against the windshield and wings leaving a quarter inch of ice on everything. Icing is the worst thing that can happen to a small airplane because, in addition to ruining your visibility and spoiling your airfoil, it increases the weight of the airplane by hundreds of pounds in seconds. It wouldn't take much ice to weigh down an old Cessna 170, foul the controls, destroy its aerodynamics, and cause it to stop flying.

The first time ice formed on the windshield, it terrified me. But then there was another clearing with no snow, and the ice fell away. At that point I was only a few miles out of Sundance, a town built in a pass through the northern Black Hills. If I could get to the east side of Sundance, the ground would fall away toward home, and I could probably drop down out of the snow and icing conditions. Besides, there was a little airstrip at Sundance, and I believed I could land there if necessary. I hit another bank of snow and came out the other side with more ice. It fell away and I could see the first buildings of the town a hundred feet below me. But it was snowing hard at Sundance, and I missed the airstrip. I still believed I could make it home if I got past the highest ground on the outskirts of Sundance. The summit was only a quarter mile away when the sky went completely white, and a sheet of ice covered the windshield. I had no choice. I banked hard and let the airplane come down, hoping a fifty-foot drop would get me out of the clouds and still keep me above the electric wires that ran along the highway.

I was scared stiff, flying by reflex and thinking that I should have known better, should have never matched that old bucket of bolts against a snowstorm. Coming down, surrounded by nothing but whiteness, I mumbled," Jesus, this is it." And finally, "I'm sorry."

Just then, a dark line appeared out my side window, and I recognized it as the long gable of the airstrip's hangar. I hauled the 170 over farther and pulled on three notches of flaps. Then I crossed the controls and slipped her for all she was worth. We fell through the cloud and popped out twenty-five feet over a pure white field. It was the Sundance airstrip, and even though it was under twelve inches of snow, it looked good to me. I cut the engine and let her come in, holding the nose out of the snow as long as I could.

An old man had heard me come over town and was plowing down the runway behind me in his four-wheel drive pickup. The airplane's main gear had lodged in a snowbank by the time he caught up to me. He pulled alongside, peering into the airplane as if I might be alien. I smiled and tried to act like I did that sort of thing all the time. But if the old man hadn't been there, I would have jumped out and kissed the snow-covered ground.

Erney and I were snowbound in the same motel that the old man took me to the last time I was stuck in Sundance. Home was just over the hill, maybe forty-five miles away, but with the first blizzard of the year raging outside, it might as well have been a thousand. We tried to watch our first television for five weeks, but we had lost our ability to stare at the moving lights and finally turned it off and read. About ten o'clock that night I looked out the front window and saw that the wind had stopped. Though there was no real reason to do it, I went out to look at Jake and Spud and Dolly.

We had gotten only a foot of snow, but the wind had blown it into piles behind the cars and buildings. The drifts were not hard because the temperature was not that cold. I looked into the back of the pickup and felt the warmth of the sleeping dogs. Dolly slept with her head behind her wing. When she woke in the morning and saw the snow, she would no doubt wonder what she was doing this far north. It had been a particularly early storm, and I was sure that it would be nice again in a few days, but she would never have been caught in it. She had probably felt it coming days before. Had this been a real migration, she would probably have been out of the storm's way. I felt foolish as I shut the back of the pickup. The streetlights in the little town were on and reflected off the new snow. At the end of the main street, centered over an old farmhouse, a hunter's moon was trying to make an appearance. It was a bright spot in the thinning clouds over the town. It reminded me of the bright spots in the sky that had lured me there once before.

The sun came up brilliantly the next morning, and by nine o'clock I was digging in the back of the truck for a pair of sunglasses. The townspeople had been clearing the streets and driveways since before sunup, but we were in no hurry to leave. Interstate 90 was still closed. We ate caramel rolls at the local café, and I couldn't help thinking that the yuppies who lived around Kris in Denver would give two dollars for a roll like that. We'd paid fifty cents and another thirty-five for the coffee.

After our breakfast we let the dogs out, then walked downtown. Already the snow was beginning to melt, but we knew that even if the county roads had been cleared, the two-mile-long driveway to my ranch would likely be blocked. (We might not get home that day, but I knew that Dolly would need to be blocked out and flown that afternoon in any case.) There was not much to do in Sundance, but we killed some time in the hardware store, then returned to the café for more coffee. We talked with ranchers and loggers who had not made it to work that morning. Just before noon, a trucker came in and said the Interstate was open.

By the time we got to the turnoff for my ranch, the county road had been plowed. I planned to spend only a week there, taking care of some business and flying Dolly nearby. Erney would stay to watch things for the winter.

Bear Butte, a sacred place, loomed four miles to the east when we turned into the driveway. The house was still two miles away, but the beginning of the driveway had been blown clear. We drove tentatively, until we came to the first drift. After looking it over, we decided we could get through it if we had enough speed. It was fifty yards long but not deep and not hard. We made it through and onto another spot the wind had cleared. The next drift was a little longer and deeper. Again, we decided that we would have a chance if we got our speed up. It would be a rough ride so we let the dogs out. Erney stood on the snowbank, holding Dolly on his fist while I drove. The pickup bucked and rolled through the worst of the drift, bogging down and finally stopping with only fifteen feet of drift to go. There were two shovels in the back, and it took only ten minutes to dig through the drift, but we were still a mile from the house.

Erney and I discussed our options. It would be impossible to turn around, but we could walk out to the county road and ask a neighbor to loan us a tractor. The other option was to keep going and take the chance of getting severely stuck. Because asking a neighbor for help did not appeal to either of us, we forged ahead. We bashed our way through two more drifts before we came to one that we could not see the end of. The sun shone powerfully, and the reflection from it was blinding. That country is stark and treeless, even when there is no snow. Now, with everything a uniform white except a few fence posts strung with dark barbed wire, the beautiful bleakness was even more striking. Erney walked ahead to find the end of the drift and came back shaking his head. He said it got shallower, but was a couple of hundred yards long. Even so, we were committed. He held Dolly, and I hit the drift as hard as I dared. I was only halfway through when the snow started coming over the hood, and we bogged down for good.

I had to crawl through the window. By the time I was out, Erney had blocked Dolly on the top of the snow and begun digging at the front tires. I was upset. "There's ten tons of snow between us and the house." I said. "We're stuck!"

Erney looked up from his work and then held the shovel for me to see. "We aren't stuck until the shovels break," he said.

We labored for two and a half hours with Bear Butte over our right shoulders, but finally we pulled the pickup onto a bare spot in front of the house. Drifts trailed off toward the southeast from all the buildings, bushes, posts, and trees. The old house, converted from a barn, stood defiantly in the landscape. When I stepped out of the truck, I looked around and remembered why I had chosen this particular place to live. You could look in any direction from the house, and not see another building. With the exception of a few fences and power lines in the distance, the time could have been a

hundred years earlier. The landscape offered an unob-
structed view. This rickety old house stood in the center
of America's grasslands.

Seventeen years before, I had decided to call this
area home. I had made the decision gravely, after
spending an entire day in a university library. From
climatic charts, demographic tables, old geological sur-
vey maps, and economic forecasts, I narrowed down
the possibilities. I took this decision very seriously because, in a way, it was the first time I had had such a
privilege. Prior to that day, I had had little to say about
where I would live. For the first time since childhood, I
was truly free. That decision was my first opportunity to
take charge, and I wasn't going to bungle it. A week
after I received a medical deferment from military service, I decided to live on the grasslands. Trees, pretty as
they are, had always seemed a barrier to my vision. I
had rewritten Joyce Kilmer's line in my mind. "I think
that I shall never see, the other side of a tree." Here, a
person could see as far as his vision would let him. It
was a place too severe to be soon overpopulated, a land
that the rest of the world might not consider worth
fighting over. And when I stepped out of the pickup
and looked at the house and landscape that most people
would say was desolate, I knew that I was home.

Dolly was blocked out in the weathering yard and
we unpacked those things needing cleaning or repair. It
was warm, and water ran off the roof, splattering into
the shrubbery that was already beginning to reappear
from the snow. By the next morning, the only hint that

there had been a blizzard would be the mud. In a few days the only reminder would be the greenness of the grass.

By five o'clock, the clothesline and the fences separating the house from the pasture were draped with tarps, sleeping bags, and the tent. The burned-out stovepipe was repaired with a piece of flashing and a few rivets from the shop. The oil in the pickup was changed, and it was time to fly Dolly.

There are five ponds within walking distance of the house. Because the roads were impassable, we decided to walk a circle that would take us by three of them. With luck we would find ducks. Dolly had been flying stronger and stronger; we would want to graduate from ducks to more difficult quarry soon.

The small birds—lark buntings, blackbirds, and meadowlarks—had already left Montana. But here, two hundred miles south, they were plentiful. A group of meadowlarks huddled on a snowbank a hundred yards in front of the house. They looked out of place there with no green and brown grass to blend into. But they knew that this snow was freak, that it wasn't going to stay on the ground long.

Dolly did not even glance at the meadowlarks when I picked her up. She did not see them as food. She would have to learn that they were catchable. But that would come later. Now we would take a walk through the melting snow and hope we could find ducks. I hooded her and strapped the hawking bag around my waist as she stood on the scale. She weighed twenty-seven and three-quarter ounces; the cold weather had brought her weight down slightly. She should be ready to hunt.

As I waited for Erney to put Spud in the kennel, I enjoyed the smell of Dolly's feathers. The smell of falcon feathers is a secret fetish of people who keep them. The smell is spicy clean, a mixture of high mountain kinnikinnick, the ocean's salt spray, and the jungles of the Yucatan. It is intoxicating. Erney and Jake caught me standing in the side yard with my eyes closed, my nose an inch from Dolly's back. Neither of them seemed to notice. Or perhaps they noticed and understood. When I looked up, Erney stood ten feet behind me staring at the ground. Jake sat beside him watching me intently and shaking slightly with excitement.

We hadn't walked twenty feet when Spud began to howl. We walked along the main draw that leads east from the buildings toward the first pond. Though the temperature had dropped again, the ground was not frozen, and the going was slower and more slippery than we had expected. We stayed on the high ground, keeping Jake at heel. At the rate we were going, it would be dark by the time we got to the third pond. There were no ducks on the first pond and I felt a little prick of fear that Dolly would not get flown that night.

The little ranch in South Dakota is not much, just a small piece of grassland with a couple of brushy draws running through it and a lot of rough land that most people would see as worthless. My banker, who is always trying to get me to plow part of it and plant crops or run more cattle, calls it a badland place. The man who used to own it, and whose defaulted loan I assumed, called it a cow-killing son of a bitch. But it suits me. Even though I have had to earn the money to make the payments by taking jobs that led me away, Erney and I were working for something we felt was important. Even if there weren't many cattle or crops, there were deer, rabbits, antelope, grouse, partridge, and ducks on this little patch of grassland, and we wanted to keep it that way. We had read every old account of this land that we could find and had determined that it was more fertile before the white man came with his plows and cattle. Our plan had always been to bring things back to what we considered full production. Recently, we had found people throughout the great plains who had the same idea.

As we moved, we looked around like two old painting conservators called to investigate an attic filled with long-forgotten oils. We commented on erosion, the deadly threat to birds and animals from barbed-wire fences set on the brink of hills, and the way the brush was coming back where we had excluded the cattle. We trudged through the wet snow to the second pond and found no ducks there either. The sun was sinking low, and the fear that Dolly would not get flown weighed me down, a responsibility not lived up to. We were hurrying toward the third pond, knowing that the light would be gone soon, when six sharp-tailed grouse purred over our heads and landed in a choke cherry thicket sixty yards away.

Jake's ears came up. Erney and I froze. Here was a dilemma. The plan had been to fly Dolly only at ducks until she was strong and confident. The sharp-tailed grouse in the brush ahead of us were as hard a quarry as there was. They would probably outfly her and perhaps discourage her. But we were running out of light and had not found any ducks. We retreated out of sight so we would not flush the grouse prematurely, and I removed Dolly's hood.

The sun was nearly down and the temperature had dropped, which should have made Dolly keen to kill and eat. Even though the countryside was covered with snow and looked different from the way she had always seen it, she left my fist immediately. Erney had been peeking at the grouse through binoculars and said that they squatted down as soon as she appeared in the sky. Jake watched her fly, whining softly. Erney and I waited.

We had been leaving her in the air longer and longer each day. I checked my watch, resolving to not flush the grouse until she had been up five minutes. She flew south until she was almost out of sight, then turned back, gaining altitude as she came. By the time she was overhead, she was several hundred feet high. Now that the grouse could see her well and were likely to stay put, we moved closer. There was a shallow impression in the prairie fifty yards from the choke cherries, and we stopped there to wait for Dolly to make one more round. She made a tight circle and set her wings to glide for a moment. It was like a signal that she was ready, and I sent Jake ahead.

He knew this game too and streaked for the thicket. Erney and I ran along behind, watching Dolly as she flew ahead to see what had excited Jake. She was directly over the thicket when Jake flushed the grouse. Sharp-tailed grouse are very different from ducks. They reach full speed before they are ten feet in the air. Without good cover to land in, they usually try to outfly the falcon. And often they succeed. But this time Dolly was in perfect position and her vertical stoop was too much for the small hen who got up last. I felt sure that the grouse would roll away from the stoop, evading a hit. But Dolly drove right through the grouse and hit it hard. It crashed into the snow with a plop, and Jake scared it back into the air just as Dolly reached the top of her pitch-up. The re-flush was not good falconry, but the timing was perfect. The grouse was rattled now and flew back toward the thicket. Dolly's second stoop knocked it down again, and this time she spun out of the air and snagged it on the ground.

I stared in disbelief. Although the style of the flight left much to be desired, Dolly had caught the first sharp-tailed grouse she had ever seen. It was disappointing that she hadn't killed it cleanly, over a point out in the open. But such aesthetics do not matter to falcons. Dolly reveled in her kill. She rolled the grouse on its back and plucked feathers proudly. Her eyes were very black and deep. She glared defiantly at Jake when he lay down in the snow hoping for a tidbit.

By then it was cold and nearly dark. I slipped in Dolly's jesses while she ate, securing her by snapping a leather bag filled with lead shot to her leash. Erney and I talked while I held a flashlight for Dolly to eat by. This was the best training Dolly could get. She had learned that grouse were good to eat and that if she caught one she would not go hungry. After awhile I switched her to the lure and slid the grouse away without her knowing it. She continued to pull at the meat on the lure that I had gauged to keep her near her flying weight, while Erney and I examined the grouse. It was a small hen and though it was too dark to see the subtle mottling of the back feathers, the whiteness of the breast was clear. Here was one of the most beautiful and admirable birds in the world. Its adaptations for cold weather are marvelous. The feet are feathered, the nostrils designed to withstand winter nights buried in snowdrifts. Their flesh is dark red and delicious. Both the legs and half of the breast of this grouse were still good. We would eat grouse that night. I tossed what was left of the head to Jake and dug my fingers into the warm body cavity of the grouse to remove its heart. Before I picked Dolly up off the lure for the long walk home, I brushed the snow away from the roots of a choke cherry bush and forced the grouse heart into the soft dirt.

That was the first night I had the dream. In it, I was on the beach where I had seen my first peregrine, on Padre Island, off the Texas coast in the Gulf of Mexico. Many birds were there. Rails waded in the marshes, meadowlarks and vesper sparrows sang in the grass, sanderlings and avocets skimmed along the beach, and great blue herons stood motionless in the shallow waters. Somewhere ahead of me was the quarry, a drake pintail. And Dolly, her jesses cut away, was just leaving my fist. We had made the migration. I had come as far as I could and was sending her on alone; but not really alone because she was joining everything that surrounded us. She left my fist for the last time and flew with all the power of a completely wild peregrine. And as I walked, I thought of the country we had traveled together, but I did not look to find her in the sky. I knew that she was there and when the pintail flushed, I did not watch it go, did not look up, or anticipate the stoop. I turned and walked away, knowing that now it was up to Dolly. In my dream I walked back to the pickup and started home. In the dream I did not look back.

The morning sun did not find me in bed contemplating the dream, but on the trail to the top of Bear Butte. I had gotten up before light and driven to the parking lot of the state park where the trails begin. Below the parking lot, in the gray morning light, several Indians, Cheyennes I suppose, moved around a sweat lodge. This was their holy place, the center of their universe and, except during the most severe months, ceremonies were common in the natural amphitheater on the south side of the butte. It is not hard to understand why this place is important to the tribes of the Great Plains. It rises a thousand feet from the prairie in the shape of a sleeping bear. It is the Mount Sinai of the Plains Indian, where the seven sacred arrows that established their law were found, and it has been the object of pilgrimages for centuries.

Not far from the sweat lodge is a particularly sacred place where Crazy Horse addressed a gathering of tribes. Every time I make the hike to the top of the butte, along the trail that winds through pine trees laden with the personal prayer bundles of hundreds of Indians, and look down on that place, I wish I had been there. I imagine the 1870s on the Great Plains and try to understand what Crazy Horse was going through. It was a time of social turmoil, tribal politics, and general confusion. The world was falling apart for the Plains Indian, and the men in power tried to cut their losses.

Great chiefs argued about how to react to the white men. Red Cloud would fight for a while, Sitting Bull would run to Canada. Many other chiefs would give in to the white man and try to convince other Indians to come to the reservation to live in frame houses and plow the fields. Finally all the chiefs would give in to one degree or another. All except Crazy Horse.

He was not really even a chief but became the symbol of resistance. Free Indians of all tribes flocked to his moving refuge camp. That huge, famous camp on the Little Big Horn was in part due to the magnetism of Crazy Horse. I have often wondered if he was one of the Indians who swam the day Custer made his strategic attack.

Mari Sandoz called him the strange man of the Oglala. He spent much of his life alone. When he was troubled he would disappear for weeks with only a horse, a blanket, and his weapons. He would return renewed, with meat for the poor of the village and perhaps an enemy scalp. Crazy Horse owned nearly nothing; he did not dress in the finery of other chiefs. He refused the flattery of the white men, scoffed at their invitations to come to Washington. He was religious, charismatic, and unswerving in his belief in his right to roam freely on the Great Plains. It has always amazed me that a man with these characteristics is not recognized as one of the truly great Americans. But he is not. Once, walking past the place where he addressed the tribes, I fantasized that the words of his speech were whispered into my ear and I was able to write them down. That, I imagined, would be all it would take. In no time those words would take their place in history.

But sitting on the top of Bear Butte, I wondered what I would really do with the knowledge of Crazy Horse's words.

The temperature had continued to rise as I made my way to the top of the butte, and I could see the draws below running with melted snow. Except for the drifts, all the snow would be gone by evening. The sky was clear, and from my vantage point I could see into Montana and Wyoming. The Blacks Hills appeared very dark to the south. I stayed on top of the butte until noon as if I were waiting for something. Actually, I was charging my batteries for the next two months. The permits necessary to transport Dolly into Nebraska and Colorado had arrived, bringing the total permits I'd received so far to fourteen. Every unit of government required me to obtain a permit from them; permits to transport Dolly, hunting licenses, game restoration stamps, and falconry licenses. I had been required to supply proof of residency to obtain most of the permits and had been told several times that I could not be a nonresident unless I was a resident of another state, and that I had not been in South Dakota enough recently to establish residency there. I was told once that I was a resident of no state and therefore the permit was denied. It occurred to me that the twenty-odd permits required to travel from Montana to Texas were a conspiracy to keep me in one place. I thought of Crazy Horse again. But unlike Crazy Horse, I would probably get all the permits eventually. They would be sent to the ranch and Erney would forward them to me at Kris's place in Denver or Jim Weaver's camp in New Mexico.

I planned to leave South Dakota soon and head

for Nebraska where the North American Falconers' Association would hold its national field meet. Later, I'd drive to Colorado, New Mexico, and finally Texas. There were a few things I needed to do before I left. I had to stop at the bank and try again to justify my loan on the ranch; and I needed to be sure the bills were paid at the feed store and the lumberyard. Still, I had the distinct feeling I was forgetting something. It was as if there was something I needed to do but was putting off. Just then a red-tailed hawk came off a rock below, set her wings and rode a thermal that had formed over the warming prairie. That is when I realized what it was I had to do.

I watched her ride the thermal, soaring effortlessly until she became a tiny spot in the blueness thousands of feet above my head. This reminded me: It was time Dolly learned to soar. The thought of it frightened me. Peregrine falcons are soaring masters. It is one of their favorite ways of hunting. They ride a thermal until they are so high that their prey cannot see them. A peregrine stoop from a soar is one of the most awesome events in nature. Dropping from perhaps a mile above the earth, they can dive at speeds approaching 238 miles per hour. The ancestors of the violet-green swallows flying around Bear Butte that day had no doubt witnessed such stoops before the peregrine became extinct in South Dakota. It was hard to believe that a peregrine could control such a stoop well enough to hit the shifty swallows. Soaring was something that Dolly had to learn to survive as a wild peregrine. It was also the best way I knew to lose a peregrine falcon.

Soaring conditions do not exist every day. Though updrafts seem to occur for a variety of reasons, the best of these currents are those produced by a variation of the earth's temperature, as in the case of a freshly plowed field situated near a body of water. The air cools over the water, becomes heavy, and pours over the plowed field. Due to solar absorption, the dark earth is warmer. The earth warms the air and creates a thermal updraft that can rise for miles off the earth with great force and speed. This type of thermal current occurs on windy *and* calm days, but calm weather increases the chances of your peregrine remaining in the vicinity. Thermal air currents are bent by the wind and so, without meaning to, a peregrine can drift miles from where it is released. It could stay thousands of feet in the air, never flap a wing, and find itself a hundred miles from the duck pond that was intended as a target. Soaring has a hypnotic effect on peregrines. They seem to relish it, sometimes more than eating, and will not come down for flushed game or the lure. This is when the peregrine is most wild, when her tie to Earth is most fragile.

So we waited, with a mixture of pleasure and dread, for the perfect day. Three days after my climb to the top of Bear Butte, I woke up to a huge yellow sun on the eastern horizon. It was warm at seven o'clock in the morning, and the wind had not come up by ten-thirty. Dolly was blocked out early, and we located a raft of gadwalls and mallards on a pond in the middle of a section of land with no fences or power wires for a half mile. At eleven o'clock I slipped Dolly's hood off as we stood beside the pickup, a quarter mile from the pond. She looked surprised. It was the first time she had been flown early on a nice day because I had been afraid of losing her in a soar. Now I was trying to make her soar.

She left the fist sluggishly. This was an un-scheduled flight for her. It was too early in the day to feel a great need to eat and too warm to be exhilarated by the air. Warm air, when it is still, has less lift than the crisp air of late afternoon, and at first Dolly flew lazily around our heads. When she saw that we were not going to produce anything interesting, she wandered off toward the north. She had not seen the pond and although Jake sat beside me as usual, she was probably confused about what she was supposed to do. She flapped off toward a ridge with the wing beat of a harrier, still not more than a 150 feet high. When she was a half mile away we brought our binoculars up and watched her. I had started the elapsed-time feature of my watch so I knew she had been in the air almost five minutes when the demeanor of her flight told us that she had lost interest in us and was flying for herself. Usually this makes a falconer dig in his bag for the lure. It is a time when you are reminded that your peregrine is indeed a *wanderer*; it can also be the last time you see her. Soaring, peregrines seem to forget all their training and revert to their essence. It is the instant that Yeats describes in "The Second Coming": "Things fall apart; the center cannot hold." It is a test of nerve to some extent. It could still be called off: You could swing the lure, and the peregrine probably would return. But that was not what we had intended to do.

I watched Dolly in the binoculars, flapping er-ratically, playing with the eddies of air over the ridge. Then I saw what I was looking for. She had been moving toward the west when, for an undetectable reason, she banked and returned to a volume of air she had just passed through. After flying east, she banked hard again, returning to the same place that had attracted her before. She had passed through a thermal and was searching for it. Finally her banking became localized and she began to form a spiral. She turned in the thermal, her wings stationary except when she was too far from the updraft and had to flap to regain her position. She moved upward at a good rate of speed. Finally she figured out the perimeters of the thermal and was able to make circle after circle without flapping. She spread her tail for more lift and soared upward at several hundred feet per minute.

At that point I began to doubt this whole venture. I tried to remember that although she was only a tiny black dot in the sky, her eyesight was infinitely better than mine. I tried not to imagine how small we must look to Dolly, how fast we were diminishing, and how many tempting things were coming into her view now that she could see a hundred miles in any direction. She could detect the slightest movement of a bird anywhere in the section of land where we had parked. It seemed impossibly optimistic to think she would have much interest in three clumsy mammals moving toward one of the seventy ponds within her vision.

But we were committed. We walked as close to the pond as we could without being seen by the ducks. They would be very jumpy since they probably did not know Dolly was above them. Even though we kept our eyes on her, and knew where to look, we occasionally lost her and it took several minutes to find her when we stopped walking. Now she was too high to see without the binoculars. The thermal had gone up fairly straight, so she was still a half mile to the north, but at that height she easily commanded the pond. The question was whether or not she would care about the ducks when they were flushed.

She would not come down until she was ready, and our job was to determine when that would be. If we flushed the ducks before she had finished her soar, she would refuse them and maybe never come down. We watched for some sign that she was prepared to hunt. Often a peregrine will break out of a thermal when it is ready for business and that is the time to flush. But sometimes it disappears, even from binoculars, and then it is guesswork. She had been up for forty-two minutes and we could barely see her with the binoculars when she broke away, lining out in our direction. This was our best chance so I told Erney to watch her while I flushed the ducks.

I lowered my binoculars and ran toward the pond. The ducks did not hesitate. They rose from the water, flying directly away from me. I watched them go. They flew easily, unhurriedly over the prairie. Then Erney jogged up beside me. He scanned the sky furiously. "She stooped," he said, "but I lost her."

Then I heard a terrible, eerie rush of air and looked toward the ducks. They were nearly a quarter mile from the pond in tight formation. The sound of the stoop intensified, and suddenly the formation dissolved. Ducks scattered in every direction and Dolly dove through the flock. Whether she hit one or not we could not tell. But the force of the stoop carried her four or five hundred feet back up into the air, and when she folded for the second time, she overtook a rattled gadwall as if it were a helium balloon.

Though Erney and I had seen this before we couldn't help being stunned. We didn't speak for a long time; mostly we shook our heads and folded and unfolded our arms. When we found Dolly I was surprised that she looked the same. She pulled at the fat duck as if nothing magical had happened. She ate this duck the way she had eaten many ducks and looked up at me as if to say that the awe in my expression was my problem, that she was at ease.

Erney collected a few more meadow mushrooms while Jake and I sat near Dolly. Since we would be traveling the next day, I let her eat all she wanted. It was the middle of the afternoon when we got back to the house and started packing. We ate meadow mushrooms and duck that night and talked only a short time before going to bed. I wanted a good night's sleep for the next day's drive, but I lay awake that night thinking about the stoop Dolly had made. I figured that she had fallen for nearly fifteen seconds, and I tried, without success, to imagine what it would be like to stoop like that. Early the next morning I was still wondering.

Erney never mentioned it, but I'm sure the sound of the Cessna 170 pulling off the alfalfa field brought him out of his own bed with a start. It was another nice morning and I trimmed the airplane to climb gradually over the grasslands. I climbed for ten minutes until I reached 5,000 feet. I re-trimmed the elevators and flew straight and level toward the pond where Dolly had flown the day before. It was not easy to find from that altitude, but I picked it out from the latticework of vegetation and draws below me. There was no way for me to tell if the ducks had returned. When I was a half mile away, I pulled the throttle back and nosed the 170 over into a sixty-degree dive. I held it like that until I could see that the ducks had returned. My rattling dive frightened them, and they flushed when I was still very high. I wanted to see what it was like to fly through them, but I was still far behind when the airspeed indicator redlined, and the airplane began to tremble. I lost my nerve and, suddenly terrified that the wings might come off, began to ease the airplane out of its pitifully clumsy stoop.

It would have been faster to drive around the Black Hills, but there was a place in the center of the Hills that I visited every autumn and this would be my last chance. With the pickup loaded again, we started up Boulder Canyon toward Deadwood. This road is in a perpetual state of disrepair and winds as it climbs the several thousand feet to the old gold mining towns. The largest hard-rock gold mine in North America is still located in Lead and is the main employer of the area. But as in most of the mining and energy-related economy of the West, the wealth doesn't seem to stay in the area. As in the oil towns, the uranium towns, and the coal towns, the promises of prosperity have never really come true and the Deadwood-Lead area of South Dakota, for all its charm and history, seems depressed and gray. The only real gold in the Black Hills is the autumn aspen leaves. And even those, on that late October day, were past their prime. I wound away from the mining towns into gravel roads and could see by the drifts of fallen aspen leaves that winter would arrive any day. I was late for my annual ruffed grouse hunt.

There is not a lot of good ruffed grouse habitat in the Black Hills because the aspen is being replaced by pine. What habitat there is does not get heavy hunting pressure and so the grouse remain tame. The place I go to is the site of an old forest fire with logging trails cut through the second growth timber. The area is hilly and the hunting hard. I never find more than a few grouse and usually only get shots at one or two, but the beauty of a hunt in the Hills at this time of year is enough to keep me coming back autumn after autumn. Because the grouse are tame they are easy for dogs to handle, perfect game for puppies. Ruffed grouse would be a good lesson for Spud.

We stopped along a logging road miles from the nearest blacktop, and I let Spud and Jake out while I pieced together the shotgun my father had given me. I ran my fingers over the chip in the stock and remembered the morning, twenty years before, when I had dropped it while trying to take it apart in the dark. The sharp pain in my left ear came back to me and I shook my head. It had been a terrible time; a time that would be nice to forget. But that was impossible because everything I was or did went back that far in my memory. It was really all that was left of my father, and in a way it had given me the freedom to start moving. If I traced the genesis of this trip with Dolly back far enough, I would find the old shutgun. I ran my finger over the stock again and then down along the barrels. It was not a fine shotgun and many times I had thought of getting a better gun. But this gun and I had a lot of history. I glanced down at Spud, who was looking up at me as if he wondered what was going on, and thought that this might be the day he would become part of that history. Then I put a handful of shells in my pocket and snapped a bell to Spud's collar so I could tell where he was in the brush. I touched him on the back of the head and told him to go on. Jake moved up to heel and we walked up the hill through the golden aspen leaves.

Spud took off and in no time his bell was out of hearing. He had never hunted in thick cover before, and he would have to learn. Though Spud liked to run, he liked people even more. Instead of trying to call him in, I sat down in a particularly thick spot and waited. Jake and I were partially hidden when Spud charged past us. I didn't say a word. In a few minutes he was back, looking a little more worried. He stood for a moment in a clearing and I could see that he was concerned that he might be lost. He charged off again, but in a moment he returned. This time he was clearly afraid that he was alone. He made several starts in different directions, then I heard him whine. That was enough. I stood up. When he saw us he bolted headlong into the thicket where we had hidden and leapt into my arms. Leaping into arms was against the rules, but I couldn't help holding him for a few seconds while he licked my face.

We tried it again. Spud moved ahead, through the aspen and the spruce. This time he stayed close and checked in frequently. We walked to the top of the rise, then followed the edge of the tallest timber. When we found an abandoned logging road, we followed it to a clearing where someone, a miner perhaps, had built a shack. It was mid-morning and the sunlight filtered through the trees in such a way that the weathered grain of the siding cast shadows on itself. It was one of thousands of little buildings that had been built in the Black Hills in the last hundred years. Nature had reclaimed the area, and now the building was only a place for a great horned owl to live.

I didn't linger at the shed. Spud was working a particularly nice edge between a group of aspens and a tiny meadow and I moved to stay up with him. But I couldn't help wondering what the builder of the shed had in mind. Had he planned to get rich in these hills? It was likely: If so, the shed was a monument to the folly of that notion. I was thinking about this when I noticed that Spud's bell had gone silent. I moved ahead quickly and looked into the juniper bushes growing along the edge. It was still in my mind that Spud might have wandered out of hearing or that he had just stopped to rest when I saw grouse droppings. Jake, still walking at heel, raised his head and tested the breeze. His tail came up and began to wag double-time. Ruffed grouse had obviously been using that area, and for the first time it seemed possible that Spud had found one and was on point. I began to search hard. I finally spotted a black and white tail pointing skyward from the center of a patch of brush.

I made Jake sit and stay, then moved toward Spud as quickly as I could without making too much noise. Finally I could see that Spud was frozen in a curved position, his head lower than his rear and turned to the side as if he had been moving perpendicular to the scent when he hit it. I shifted around so that the grouse was more likely to flush into the open. When I was within five feet of Spud's nose, I stopped and looked hard into the grass and brush. For a long time I saw nothing, then I caught the flick of the grouse's tail and heard it make a putt-putt sound. The sound made Spud's ears come up even higher, and he swelled with excitement but didn't move. It was proof that his nose had not lied to him. "Easy," I said, sliding shells into the twenty-gauge. I closed the gun and moved to flank the grouse.

Even though I knew that it was ready to fly, the sound of its wings startled me. Spud jumped in as the grouse pounded free of the brush. It turned sharply to miss a pine tree and careened back toward the shed. It was an easy shot and it crumpled not far from where Jake waited. The sound of the shotgun and the falling grouse were too much. Jake broke and scooped up the grouse before it had stopped rolling. Spud, being inexperienced, had not watched the bird down and ran off frantically in the wrong direction. I stepped into the clearing and met Jake who brought the grouse to me posthaste, his tail arched and his head high and proud.

I knelt and took the bird. The big dog wiggled all over, then got a grip on himself and regained his dignity by lying down as I inspected the grouse. Spud returned and nosed the bird as I turned it in my hands. I marveled at the delicate brown feathers of its neck, spread the tail and saw by the continuous black band that it was a male. It was probably a bird of the year, recently dispersed from its family group. Somewhere close, there was a log that this bird would have used to drum in females in the spring. Now the log would be used by another grouse. I made a note to myself to come back in late April and listen to the thmm-thmm-thmm. Then I spread the wings and tried to grasp the phenomenon of evolution that had produced this bird. These cup-shaped wings, pounding against a log, could call a female from a great distance, yet the sound was some-how ventriloquistic and hard for predators to find. The drumming is also produced at forty cycles a second, well within the auditory range of the grouse but too low to be heard by the great horned owl that probably lived near the old shed. Nature is a process of selection; everything fits at least as snugly as the works of a watch. The grouse whose wings beat at fifty cycles a second were all gone, and so were the people who built the shed.

The three of us walked back to the truck and I gave Spud and Jake a drink of water. Dolly stood on her perch. I could see by the bulge at her neck that there was a little duck still in her crop from the day before. She would not be interested in flying that afternoon. That was fine, since I wanted to camp near the North Platte and try her the next day in Nebraska. It was afternoon by then and had begun to cloud up. After I cleaned the grouse, we loaded up and made our way to the blacktop road. By the time we left the Black Hills the clouds were dark, and it looked like snow. When I returned in seven weeks, the Hills would be buried under four-foot drifts. We were leaving just in time.

Because it is so sad I don't visit Fort Robinson, Nebraska, very often. But since it was on my way I decided to drive past. It was a pilgrimage I did not relish, a little like a Christian going alone to Calvary, complete with the outrage of a senseless murder but without the neat justification that it was done for our salvation. Fort Robinson is the place Crazy Horse was murdered. In the latter 1870s it was a military post, established to protect whites moving into the Black Hills. It was also a depot for gathering and shipping the Indians to reservation compounds. The beauty of the land where the fort stands hides the shame of its history.

It was evening when I reached the pine-covered ridge northwest of the fort. I stopped the pickup and looked at the valley below, trying to imagine what it must have been like when thousands of Sioux were loosely held there by the soldiers of the fort. The military had known just how to manipulate the Sioux. They had turned many chiefs against each other and ruled them through rumor and intrigue. All the other Indians had already surrendered before Crazy Horse could be convinced to come into the fort.

Indian emissaries, chiefs who commanded respect, were sent out with pack trains of food and supplies to the starving camp of Crazy Horse. They pleaded with him to give up his freedom and join the others in captivity. He was promised his own agency for his people and told that they would be allowed to hunt in the autumn for their winter meat. It was the offer of a yearly hunt, and the fact that his people were starving to death, that convinced Crazy Horse. He was the last of the free Sioux, and all of the agency Indians turned out to watch his tattered but proud people march along the valley beneath my truck.

He was the most respected of all the Indians then. Mari Sandoz, in *Strange Man of the Oglala*, quotes an officer who watched the procession as saying, "By God! This is a triumphal march, not a surrender." What made Crazy Horse triumphal was his wildness, his unconquerable freedom. The soldiers hated and feared him for it. Indians loved him for it, but some envied him because even in captivity he refused to give up. Crazy Horse never received the agency he was promised and was not allowed an autumn hunt. He was murdered a few months after his arrival, as the soldiers tried to put him in chains. Just who killed him is not clear. But it is clear that his death was humiliating, coming at the hands of frightened, jealous people within the walls of the fort. The names of the men who plunged the knives or bayonets into him and the names of those who held him are lost. It seems likely that they were both white and Indian. Looking down on the fort from the ridge, I could imagine the claustrophobia of Crazy Horse's last moments and knew that it was envy that killed him. It seemed to me that killing Crazy Horse was an act very much like that of a farmer who, after witnessing a peregrine falcon stoop from the heavens to catch a duck, creeps up on it while it feeds and kills it with a rusty pitch fork.

I did not go near the fort. I drove around it and headed south. By the time I reached Alliance it was very dark. I gassed up at a 7-Eleven and drove to the Crescent Lake Wildlife Refuge. Spud and Jake checked the area out while I fried the ruffed grouse in an iron skillet over the Coleman stove. I ate until I could hold no more, then unrolled my sleeping bag and pad on the ground and slid the .357 under my pillow. Before I turned in, I weighed Dolly. Because she had eaten a lot of duck the afternoon before, I had not fed her all day. My hope was that after a day without food her weight would be right for flying her at pheasants or grouse. She weighed twenty-nine and a half ounces. That was too much, but it was cold and she would burn more calories than usual. She would be close to the right weight by the next afternoon.

In the morning I put the coffee on the stove and walked until I could see the water of Crescent Lake. A large flock of sandhill cranes stood near the edge, and I scanned them with binoculars, hoping to see a whooping crane among them, but had no luck. On the other side of the water was a flock of Canada geese. It was unlikely but not impossible that they were the same flock that had shared the pond with us in Montana.

It was now the first week in November and although the ponds in Montana were frozen, Nebraska's Crescent Lake was frantic with life. I could see five species of ducks, the cranes, the geese, red-wing blackbirds and several species of shore birds. For some birds, this would be as far south as they would go. But the majority would move on, like us, into Colorado, New Mexico, and Texas. A few—Dolly, perhaps, among them—would go on to Central America.

The morning was cool, but the bright sun promised to warm the day, insuring that any ice formed during the night would not last. It was a clear, blue prairie day with the wind already picking up. I went back to my little camp, blocked Dolly out, turned Spud and Jake loose and poured a cup of coffee. After finishing my first cup, I went to the lake and scooped a bucket of water for Dolly's bath. There were three weeks until the North American Falconers' field meet would be held in Kearney, Nebraska, and I planned to spend that time flying Dolly in the pastures and grain fields flanking the North Platte River. Unless the weather turned bad, I could expect to find plenty of game for her. If the Indian summer lasted, I would be able to stay long enough to see a few old friends at the field meet.

My plan was to join Kent Carnie and Jim Weaver in New Mexico in any case. So if the weather forced me out of Nebraska I would go to Colorado and spend the extra time with Kris. The longer I was out, the better that sounded.

I sat and watched Dolly take her bath, and the more I sat, the more I liked the place we had found. By the time Dolly jumped from the bath pan to her perch and spread her feathers to dry, I had decided to stay awhile. I began unloading and setting up camp. Spud and Jake returned from a swim in the lake and I tied them up so that when we were ready to go hunting, they would be around to go along. Before Dolly's feathers were completely dry and preened, the camp was livable and the dogs snoozed contentedly in the afternoon sunlight. I sat down in my chair with the tent shielding me from the breeze and was asleep in seconds.

I awoke to the sound of Dolly's bells. It was late, time we were out hunting and Dolly bated with anticipation. When I weighed her, she was a half-ounce heavier than usual, but late in the day this was all right. I fixed the radio transmitters to her legs and loaded Dolly,

Spud, and Jake into the back of the pickup. Because the country was new to me we should have been out earlier, looking for ponds or likely places to run Spud in search of pheasants or grouse. I drove too fast, thinking that there was a good chance that we would not find anything until it was too late. The lake was much too large, but I thought certainly there would be a pond close by with ducks. I found none. The more I looked and found nothing, the more irritated I became, the faster I drove and, no doubt, the more game I missed. Finally I began to lose hope. I had forgotton that the days were shorter in Nebraska because of the latitude. The sun had begun to set and in a few minutes it would be too dark to fly.

Suddenly, a rooster pheasant sailed across the dirt road ahead of us and into a five-acre swale surrounded by harvested cornfields. If we had more time I would have driven right past. Pheasants are notorious runners and can be very hard to locate. The chances of us finding the rooster were only fair. But on the other hand, the pheasant was obviously going to roost for the night and there was a good chance that there were more pheasants in the low marshy grass. I decided to take the risk and pulled the pickup off the road.

Because it was late, cool, and nearly dark, Dolly flew hard, pumping her wings without stopping until she was very high overhead. She was in such good position that she commanded most of the swale, and I decided to let both dogs out. There was only one patch of cover that a pheasant could fly to, a line of trees a half mile away with nothing but harvested corn in between. Pheasants are not good long-distance flyers and I was sure that Dolly could overtake one before it reached the trees. We walked slowly from one end to the other, planning to flush the pheasants out toward the trees. The sun sank lower and the dogs crisscrossed in front of me, but no pheasants came up.

By the time we reached the other end of the swale, it was nearly too dark to see Dolly. Apparently we had missed the rooster. Jake, who had stuck closer to me, sniffed hard at the patches along the end of the swale, likely places for the rooster to have run into. I called Spud in, trying to encourage him to do the same, but he ran frantically back into the harvested corn. I lost my temper and screamed at him to come back and look for the pheasant. He returned and sniffed around for a few seconds while I debated calling Dolly down to the lure, but in no time Spud was back out in the corn stubble. I had resolved to call Dolly down and then catch Spud and punish him, when he froze on point in the stubble. It was only a flash point because the rooster sprang into flight, heading for the trees immediately, and I lost sight of both him and Dolly in the last rays of sunlight.

The first thing that I did was to call Spud in and apologize to him. Being a dog, he forgave my lack of faith without question. Then we waited to see if Dolly would come back. I rated the chances of her catching the rooster at fifty-fifty and although it would have been nice for Dolly to make a kill, I would have been happy to see her coming back. The thought of her out in the open, feeding on a pheasant in the dark, frightened me. She would be difficult to find and night is a dangerous time for a peregrine on the ground.

She did not come back and after five minutes it

was too dark for her to fly. We returned to the pickup to get the telemetry receiver. I left Spud in the pickup because he was too rambunctious for a night search in strange country. Jake stuck close to me and, though his black coat made him invisible in the night, it was nice to know that he was there. I got a signal immediately and the rhythmic beep-beep was reassuring. As long as there is a signal, the falcon does not seem to be lost. The signal is directional, and it indicated that Dolly was somewhere near the small grove of trees that the pheasant had probably tried to reach. As Jake and I started across the cornfield, I thought how comforting the beeping of the transmitter was. Silence would be the worst sound possible. Then I heard another sound, and a chill ran up my back. I turned the receiver off and identified the bass tones of a great horned owl. Suddenly I wanted silence. But the hoots continued and it was clear that they were coming from the same direction as the transmitter signal.

I quickened my pace, listening first to the owl and then to the receiver. Dolly was not moving, which might mean that she had caught the pheasant. But the owl was not moving either, which might mean it had caught Dolly. Peregrines cannot see well at night, and they are preyed upon ruthlessly by great horned owls. In the daylight peregrines will kill great horned owls, if given a chance, but a peregrine wrestling a pheasant in the dark is defenseless against a great horned owl. I had taken the flashlight from the hawking bag when we left the pickup. Now I turned it on hoping it might frighten the owl. I could just make out the silhouette of the trees against the sky when a second owl began to hoot. This was not unusual; great horned owls are often found in pairs or family groups. The line of trees was a likely nesting territory and because great horned owls do not move much, they probably used it all year long. Over the years the owls of that tree grove might have caught many young falcons and small hawks they saw catch game just at dark. Only birds of prey with experience would recognize the danger hidden in the trees.

The receiver indicated that we were close to Dolly, or what was left of her. Enough time had elapsed that the owls could have made a meal of her, and I was sick as I searched the ground with the flashlight. I cast the beam over the ground where Dolly should have been but saw nothing. Then I rechecked the receiver, and again, it indicated that I was very near the transmitter. For one terrible second it occurred to me that the owls had eaten part of her and carried the rest of her to the trees, leaving only the leg with the transmitter. I ran the flashlight beam over the ground again and saw nothing. The owls continued to mock me from the trees. Then I noticed Jake raise his head and smell the air. I took a couple more steps and he sat down, the way he was trained to react when Dolly was on the lure or a kill. I looked intensely on a line directly into the breeze from his nose, took another step, and heard a hawk bell. Dolly was less than five feet in front of me. She lay perfectly flat, her wings outstretched and her head turned to the side. For an instant I thought she was dead. But one dark eye looked upward at me and glistened at the edge of the flashlight beam. She adjusted as I approached and the bell sounded faintly.

When I sat beside her she stood, revealing the

rooster pheasant. It was dead, but not a feather was out
of place. Probably Dolly had seen the owls in the trees
just after she killed the pheasant. She had lain down so
the owls would not see her or the pheasant. Her instincts had saved her, and I did not dwell on how close it
had been. I wondered what she had felt like, lying on
her face in the corn stubble knowing that death was out
there in the blackness and that her only chance was to
remain absolutely still until dawn. Now, with Jake and I
near, and the pheasant illuminated by the flashlight,
she began to eat very much like normal. But I looked
closely. Her eyes were slightly deeper, her feathers
tighter, and her grip on the pheasant more intense. In
some immeasurable way this was a different peregrine
from the one who had disappeared into the dusk an
hour before.

We hunted the sandhills and grasslands of
Nebraska for three weeks. The weather held, and on the
last day of the North American Falconers' field meet we
rolled into Kearney. It was the first field meet I had
attended in nearly twenty years. I had gone off to fly my
falcons by myself and had not been active in the North
American Falconers' Association. I had shied away from
organizations and groups of people. But NAFA had
become the legislative lobby for birds and prey, and it
was largely through its efforts that falconry and the
natural history of birds of prey had become understood
and accepted by the general public.

When I began to keep falcons, they were considered vermin, and many states paid bounties for killing
them. In those days falconers were considered the luna-

tic fringe. Falconry was not understood, and falconers were unfairly treated by many government agencies and wildlife organizations. But falconers fought for a basic understanding of predator-prey relationships, and finally laws protecting birds of prey were passed and falconry became established as a proper field sport. In the light of biological fact, falconry's detractors were embarrassed.

I felt a little uneasy as I walked past the people who had fought my battles for me in Washington and in state capitals across the country. Though I had contributed in my own way, these were the people who had fought in the trenches to outlaw the killing of birds of prey, the people who perfected captive breeding of hawks and falcons and supplied the energy to restore the peregrine falcon in North America.

The gathering in Kearney was very different from the last meet I had attended and underscored the fact that falconry had come of age. The headquarters was a motel on the edge of town, and before I had even parked the pickup I began to see falcons. There was a weathering yard set up in back of the motel, and inside it were hawks and falcons of every description. A full-time supervisor checked people in and out of the weathering yard. There were strict rules about feeding birds in sight of other birds, blocking birds too close to each other's, and admittance of unauthorized persons. I did not plan to fly Dolly at the meet, so I had fed her and left her in the pickup with the dogs, where she was at home. What I had come here for was a break, to see a few friends, and to get a shower.

As I walked to the lobby to register, I noticed

license plates from states on both coasts and throughout the Midwest. There were many more falcons than there had been at the meets I remembered. Captive breeding had made fine birds available to a large number of falconers. The blocks, falconry gloves, hoods, and car perches that I passed were far superior to what had been the norm twenty years before. There were a great number of young people, and quite a few women. These were average Americans: factory workers, professionals, laborers, civil servants. They looked happy. I did not see the silent, dark-eyed, asocial young men I remembered from the days when falconry was quasi-legal.

After my bath, I looked for Jim Weaver. I had gotten a message that his longtime woman companion, Phyllis Dague, needed a ride to the airport in Denver the next day. As the president of the North American Falconers' Association, Jim was one of the people responsible for that organization's prominence as a national force in conservation. I had met Jim on the winter plains of South Dakota many years before. He was retired then and planned to travel to the northern plains with his gyrfalcon until he was too old to get around. But it hadn't worked out that way. Within a year the decline of the peregrine had forced Tom Cade to found the Peregrine Fund at Cornell University, and Jim was asked to manage it. Those were the days when raising peregrine falcons for release was considered unfeasible and the Peregrine Fund was short of capital. The truth may well be that the money Jim Weaver had salted away for retirement was one of the first large contributions to the Peregrine Fund.

For years Jim was busy with the reintroduction of peregrines; later he became president of NAFA. He never got to retire to the northern plains and fly his falcons, but he spent a lot of time there, and for years I would run into him regularly. I would find him, without warning, sleeping in my driveway. Once I found him on a back road in North Dakota on a very cold day, sitting in his pickup with his falcon blocked outside, turning the pages of a book while wearing heavy, wolf-hide mittens. We had shared many camps and in recent years had hawked together regularly in New Mexico. I knew that he was at the meet because I had seen his dual-wheeled three-quarter-ton pickup with horse trailer (complete with dressing room and dog kennels) parked behind the motel. His horse was probably stabled out of town. I had peeked in the trailer and seen that it was crammed full of boots, gun cases, falconry equipment, and horse tack. He was obviously heading for New Mexico as soon as he finished his official duties at the meet.

As it turned out, Jim's official duties kept him busy. I watched him smiling as he handed out awards and shook hands at the banquet that night. It was a good front, but I knew that all he wanted was to get away and be alone with his falcon. I relaxed, drank some whiskey, and watched a group of young falconers from California perform a skit in which they made fun of their own inability to teach their falcons to catch grouse. People had a good time. There was a slide show of migrating peregrines with wonderful music. Finally, I went to sleep on the clean sheets of the motel room bed. My head was filled with the peregrines of the slide show, and after I fell asleep the dream came to me again. It was very much the same: The beach on Padre Island, thousands of birds, and the drake pintail on a pond in front of us. The sea breeze blew salty against my face, and Dolly flew as strong as a wild peregrine. But this time she found a thermal and soared. She was a tiny speck when the pintail flushed and I turned and walked away from the pond.

In the morning I met Jim and Phyllis for breakfast. The meet was over, but still people came up to Jim with questions and comments. He was tired of being president. A week of high profile had been enough. It would be a long haul to New Mexico pulling a horse trailer and a ton of equipment, and he dreaded it. When we opened the back of the trailer, an avalanche of tools and gear crashed onto the asphalt. He had to dig through a pile of saddles and bags of dog food to find Phyllis's suitcase. We moved almost everything in the bed of his pickup to find a crate with a pair of mounted prairie chickens inside that Phyllis had to take back to Ithaca. By the time we finished with the transfer, Jim was exasperated.

He looked out toward the cornfield behind the motel. "It didn't used to be this complicated," he said. Phyllis was watching him by now, shaking her head. "What I should do is get rid of all this stuff," he said wistfully. "Should take it all out there in that field and make a pile." Now he was talking to himself. "The pickup, the horse trailer, all that junk." He looked down at his shirt. "These Eddie Bauer clothes," he said. "The dogs could run to New Mexico. Put it all in a pile and pour gas on it. I should just put my falcon on my fist and throw a match on the pile. Then climb on that horse, bareback and naked, and ride to New Mexico."

Phyllis rolled her eyes and shook her head again. "It's been a rough week," she said. "A rough year. He needs this vacation."

"Just pour gas on all of it," Jim was saying.

"See you in a month or so," Phyllis said.

Jim was still standing in the parking lot of the motel when we pulled out for Denver. He planned to get to his camp in New Mexico in one shot, a hard drive. But Phyllis wasn't worried. "He needs the trip," she said. "Needs to be alone." They had been together for seventeen years and Jim had spent a lot of that time both camping alone all over the world and lobbying for conservation issues in Washington. Somehow Phyllis had learned to live with it. They had a strange but good relationship.

Thinking about that relationship made me think of Kris. I had not seen her for months and had tried not to think about it. But now, driving down Interstate 70 toward Denver, I found that there was no reason not to let my mind drift a little. I would be at Kris's house in a matter of hours. Jake would be one happy dog. I could get a cup of espresso and stay in bed until nine o'clock. We could go out to see a play or a movie. There were duck ponds close to Denver and Dolly could fly every day. By the time the cities of Colorado's front range began to spring up around us, I was feeling terrible fatigue and did not notice that a thick, gray, winter sky loomed over the snowcapped Rocky Mountains.

LLANO
ESTACADO

———————

*T*here were thousands of Canada geese around Fort Collins. They flew over the highway, settling in great dark swirls into the cornfields on either side. With the geese were large ducks, mallards, and pintails, who landed in the corn like shadows of the Canadas. The migration had come this far. I rolled down the window and the honking of geese drowned out the sound of the highway. Then we were in Denver, and the crush of the city surrounded us.

We were rushed at Stapleton Airport and there was no time to park. Crowds of people, intent on assaulting the fresh snow in the mountains, pushed out of the doors carrying tons of skiing equipment. I helped Phyllis flag down a skycap, and then a policeman started toward my illegally parked pickup. We hugged each other, and although she didn't say it she was thinking she'd like to go along with me, following the Rocky Mountains southward until I met up with Jim on the Llano Estacado. One last squeeze and she was gone, into the belly of the airport, and I jumped into the pickup before I got a ticket. Horns sounded as I pulled out into the traffic, and I rolled the window up against the smell of exhaust fumes.

Kris was an anesthesiology resident at the University of Colorado Hospital. She was working that month with heart surgeons. Her job was to put people to sleep, keep them alive while a machine performed the duties of the heart that was being repaired, and then bring them back to consciousness. She worked long hours in the operating room, so she lived near the hospital in an old residential area of Denver not far from Washington Park. When we crossed Cherry Creek, I was struck by the contrast between what that area had been for thousands of years and what it had become in the last fifty. Cherry Creek, situated on the edge of the mountains, had once been a winter gathering place for all kinds of animals. Elk and deer came there to join beaver and scores of prairie dwellers. Much later, men began to winter in that sheltered, fertile area. Centuries later, a town began to grow to the west. Now Cherry Creek is little more than water diverted down a concrete channel, no longer a creek at all. It has become synonymous with high fashion and society, a perfect example of what has happened so often in areas of such astounding beauty. It is the old irony. People come to these places because of the beauty, and their coming destroys all traces of what brought them in the first place. In a way that is the story of Colorado, and it is symbolized by the ski industry, which sells speed as if it had something to do with experiencing nature.

Wolf Creek Pass is in the mountains southwest of Denver. It is one of the most lovely areas in North America, and peregrine falcons nested there for centuries. Like almost all the peregrines in Colorado, they disappeared as a result of DDT. I helped release captive-bred peregrines on the cliffs above Wolf Creek Pass for several years, until they once again nested above the wide lush valley. From the top of those cliffs you can see one of Colorado's most pristine drainages. At the lower end of that drainage, near the highway, is the headquarters of the development company that plans to turn it all into a ski resort. They have built a little inn with a dining room, a bar, and rooms to rent to prospective investors.

One day, several weeks after we had released four peregrines from a hack box on the cliff, I stopped at the developemnt headquarters to make a telephone call. I had been to the top of the cliff several times that day checking on the peregrines, and I was hot and sweaty. After I made my call, I tried to sit in the corner of the bar and be alone, but a smiling young woman approached me and sat down. She was beside herself with awe. She said she had never been in such a beautiful place. I agreed, and we looked out the window at the cliff where the young peregrines, far too high for us to see, had begun to make their first hunting flights. She explained that she was there from Los Angeles to invest money for her family. She pointed out the window at the hillside across the valley and said that was where she was going to build her condominium. Below and downstream she planned to buy two more lots for her brothers. She stood up and went to the window so she could show me how convenient the shopping area would be to their lots. There would be single-family dwellings all along one side of the valley and roads and sewers were included in the price of the lots. The area she pointed to supported the food base for the peregrines on the cliff and for every living thing for miles. It would be ruined by this development, which was being built directly in the migration path of thousands of elk, cutting them off from their wintering grounds and, ultimately, survival.

This woman was attractive and I watched her as she leaned wistfully against the window frame. It crossed my mind that I could get a room, take a shower, maybe ask this woman to dinner. A small band of elk grazed high on the slope across the valley, and I pointed them out to her. At first she did not see them and didn't believe me. Finally she saw them and her excitement left her nearly speechless. She stared at the elk for a long time before she began to talk again. She had lived her whole life in Los Angeles and had never seen live elk before. Elk hunters, she said, were trying to stop the development. She could not understand how anyone could hunt elk. She could never kill something that beautiful, she loved the out-of-doors too much. She said that just being there along Wolf Creek was invigorating to her because it was so wild and natural. I have often wondered what she thought when she turned from the window with the enthusiasm and innocence of a little girl, to find that I was gone.

🌿

Slaves to their instincts, some birds were still trying to use the Cherry Creek area. A small vee of geese set their wings and sank behind locust trees on their way to Washington Park. As I turned onto University Boulevard, a sharp-shinned hawk shot across the busy highway in hot pursuit of a starling. A pair of magpies squawked from the trees in Kris's backyard. Because Kris often worked until nine or ten o'clock, I was surprised to see her car parked in the alley. There was still an hour of light and the backyard looked safe so I blocked Dolly out before I went into the house. Jake knew where he was and leapt high in the air at the back door. When I let him in, he charged as if the house might harbor a duck in need of retrieving. But he was after Kris. They met in the kitchen and embraced in a din of squeals and yips. Spud could see that this lady liked dogs, so he pressed against her leg as she made a fuss over Jake. I had to wait my turn.

But the wait was worth it. I had not realized how much I had missed the closeness of a woman until Kris buried her head against my chest and held me tightly. Then I noticed the delicate smell of the baking brioche dough that surrounded the Beef Wellington. Now Erney is a fine cook, but he would have to be described as a camp cook. Kris, on the other hand, could cook in a palace. It is one of her attributes, one of the many things that made me forget, temporarily, that I was migrating.

I had forgotten about eating like that. We started with shrimp bisque and a bottle of cabernet sauvignon. With the Beef Wellington we had asparagus, steamed lightly with cream sauce. The beef was medium rare throughout and the Madeira sauce was plentiful. Then came the poached pears and a split of Muscat Canelli.

Dolly was safe in the back of her pickup and the dogs lay comfortably in front of the fireplace. We took our brandies into the living room and snuggled together on the couch. We didn't talk. I tasted the brandy, smelled Kris's hair, and thought that no one had ever enjoyed an evening more. Spud rolled over and looked up at us, then slowly got to his feet and laid his head on Kris's lap. I was reminded of something Robert Graves once told a visitor. "The political and social confusion of the last three thousand years has been entirely due to man's revolt against woman as a priestess of the natural magic, and his defeat of wisdom by the use of intellect."

※

Tens of thousands of ducks winter within a hundred miles of Denver. They spend the nights on the large ice-free reservoirs that supply the cities with water to drink and the farmers with water to irrigate, and they feed in the cornfields and wheat fields along the front range, the eastern slope of the Rockies. They also use smaller ponds that can be hunted with a falcon. The drawback is that gun hunters also use these ponds. Because a few gun hunters are not discriminating enough to tell a peregrine falcon from a duck, it is hazardous to turn a falcon loose. You must find ponds where there are ducks and where the falcon is safe. Sometimes this means traveling a great distance from the population centers, and sometimes this means hunting ducks inside the city limits where guns are not allowed.

I left Kris's house at noon the next day. A friend who had been raised in Denver and flown falcons there once took me for a ride around the city and showed me the old ponds that had been good for him. That had been four years before and, even then, we had found that several of his best ponds had become parking lots for office buildings. He could not believe it. I drove to the ponds he had showed me and found that they had all met similar fates. There was one that still existed as a pond but now was incorporated into a golf course and, even though it was November and chilly, two cartloads of golfers scurried over the grass not far from the pond. I drove farther from the city. The only ducks I saw on a safe pond were a group of mallards on the sewage lagoon for the suburb town of Parker. I drove farther out, finding ponds but no ducks. Several times I came across gun hunters. It was late afternoon when desperation drove me to return to the Parker sewage lagoon.

For ten minutes I surveyed the situation with binoculars from the hill above the lagoon. There were actually three ponds, perhaps 150 feet by seventy-five. There were thirty or forty mallards on one of the ponds; after watching for a while, I saw a raft of smaller ducks swim out from the bank of another. Had the situation been more remote, it would have been ideal. But this was a highly regulated area, with large "no trespassing" signs wired to an eight-foot-high chain-link fence. Still, it was the only flyable pond I had found.

I drove up the single-lane service road toward the lagoon. It was obviously intended only for official use and there was no other exit. My little pickup with its camper and out-of-state license plates certainly did not look official, but it was past five o'clock and I argued to myself that the city sewage people had quit for the day. I stopped the pickup in a low spot very near the fence. We were not hidden, but somehow I thought the low spot would make us less obtrusive to citizens driving past their city sewage lagoon. I started to read the sign

on the fence but gave up when I came to the word
PROSECUTION.

Because this was strictly a duck hunt, I had left
Spud at Kris's, and when I opened the back of the truck,
Jake's big square head popped out. He panted with
excitement and on an impulse I held a finger to my lips
and made a shushing sound. Before I brought Dolly
out, I looked in all directions as nonchalantly as possible. The coast was clear. Off with the hood, into the air,
and I tried to pretend that I didn't notice the large dark
peregrine falcon beginning to mount above me. I leaned
against the pickup and looked closely at the fence. It
would not be hard for me to climb up one of the metal
posts, scramble over the barbed wire, and jump to the
ground on the other side, but getting Jake inside might
be more difficult. I thought about leaving him behind,
but by now he was watching Dolly pumping crisply
upward, and he shook with excitement. I couldn't leave
him. There was a chance I could hold the bottom of the
fence up high enough for him to crawl under.

We watched for another few minutes, and I could
hear the mallards quacking their disapproval just out of
our sight. When Dolly reached her pitch and set her
wings, I waved Jake out of the pickup and sprinted for
the fence. Until then, I figured that I could talk myself
out of a trespass charge. Once I started over the fence, it
was clear that I was willfully breaking the law, so I
wanted to be as quick as possible. When I started to
climb, Jake became frantic. He raced back and forth,
barked, dug at the bottom of the fence. By the time I hit
the ground on the other side, he was biting at the heavy
chain link. I managed to pull the fence up a few inches

and Jake, lying on his side and squirming violently, forced his way under. When I turned and started to jog toward the pond, I realized why no ducks were using the third pond. It was nearly raw sewage and I hoped that Jake would have the good sense not to dive in.

Of course Jake knew exactly what he was doing. We jogged past the fetid water toward the two cleaner ponds. When I saw the mallards, I sent Jake ahead, and they came off the water into the wind and turned to go with it. Dolly drove one into the tangle of broken machinery fifty yards outside the lagoon compound and settled on top of it. Without stopping I jogged back to the corner of the fence. Jake was right behind and seemed to know that he had to wait for me to pull the fence up. When he was under, I started over, but half-way up, I saw a car coming down the service road toward us.

I pulled myself over the barbed wire and dropped. When the car pulled up alongside the pickup I was leaning against it, pretending I hadn't seen the man coming. Dolly was eating her duck, out of sight, so I thought it best to lie.

"Just passing through," I told the man in the car with the seal of the town of Parker, Colorado, on the door. "Thought this would be a good place to let my dog out for a while." Luckily, the man had not seen me scaling his fence. He was a happy city employee, just out to check something in the small building beside the lagoon. I hope that it would not take too long. Dolly had probably plucked most of the body feathers by now and would start eating soon. If she ate too much, she would not feel like flying the next day.

The man wanted to talk. He has seen my South Dakota license plate and asked exactly where I was from. I tried to be polite, and at the same time discourage too much conversation. Jake lay at my feet. He was wet and didn't look at all like a dog that had just been let out of a pickup after a long ride. Finally, the man unlocked the gate and drove into the compound to do his work. He disappeared inside the little building, but there was no way that I could get to Dolly to pick her up without taking a chance that he would see us. The pile of machinery that she had landed in probably belonged to the city, and I was sure that the sewer man would not appreciate me fumbling around it. I waited, worrying all the time that Dolly would eat too much. If I waited too long, she might even get her fill, fly away, and be almost impossible to get back. I determined that I would wait another few minutes and then, PROSECUTION or not, go and pick her up.

The sewer man came out of the building, got slowly into his car, drove through the gate, got out, locked the gate, and came back to park beside my pickup. "Been a nice day," he said. I nodded. "Damndest thing. Must be a cold front coming through. This is the first day in three weeks that there haven't been ducks on the ponds."

"No," I said. "You mean ducks use those ponds?"

He smiled and nodded his head as if he were imparting the knowledge of a great naturalist. "All the time," he said. "I think they like shit."

I wanted him to leave but couldn't let that pass. "Sure they don't use this because most of their natural ponds have been destroyed?"

He thought for a minute, then shook his head. "No," he said. "Wild animals seem to have a natural attraction for human shit."

I smiled my most wooden smile and resolved not to speak again until this man went away. Finally he put the car in gear and began to roll away. "Have a nice day," he said.

Jake and I watched until he turned onto the highway, then sprinted to Dolly. She had already eaten too much duck. I picked her up as quickly as possible and we left the Parker sewer lagoon. She would be too heavy to fly the next day. But I tried to look at the bright side: It would give me a day to scout a better place to fly her. I had already decided that I would not fly her at the Parker sewage lagoon again unless it was an absolute necessity.

It had only been dark for a little while when we arrived at Kris's house. Jake had a less than pleasant odor so I left him outside. I found Kris watching the news with Spud curled up on her lap.

"He crawled up here on his own," she said. "First his head, then a paw, then two paws, and before I knew it, he was asleep. I don't even know this dog."

"He has a problem," I said.

"He's heavy," she said and pushed him off. She stood up and put her arms around my neck. "How did Dolly do?" Then, "What's that smell?"

※

Because Kris had to be the first person in the operating room, she left the house at 5:30 A.M. I got up with her and sat drinking coffee as she got ready for work. She talked about the cases that were scheduled for that day: open-heart surgery, new valves, cleaning arteries. The last thing she said before she left was that she hoped Dolly flew well that day. As I unwrapped the *Denver Post*, I could not help comparing her day to mine. It must be nice, I thought, to know for sure that every day you were doing something important.

I read an article in the newspaper about a man who was very mad at the animal-control people. He had called them to come out to his small suburban horse ranch to get rid of a beaver that had dammed up the irrigation ditch in front of his house. Denver is surrounded by little acreages where people live, along with a few horses, within easy commuting distance of their jobs in the city. In this case, the irrigation ditch winds through an entire district of these "hobby ranches" from an inlet point that takes water from the South Platte River. The beaver had done what was natural: made his way down what seemed to be a stream splitting off his ancestral South Platte River and begun to do what beavers do. He cut the willows that grew beside the irrigation ditch and built a dam.

The man who owned the land along the ditch did what was natural too. He tried to discourage the beaver from impounding the water. He tore down the dam. The beaver rebuilt. The dam was removed again and so on, until the man got disgusted and called the government agency that was supposed to take care of these things. These men had seen this before. They were realists. They got rid of the beaver by trapping it in the most efficient trap they had. The beaver died. The man who had called them was incensed. In the newspaper article, he chastised the animal-control people for their insensitivity. It seemed to him that the beaver should have been live-trapped and moved to another location. His neighbors sided with him. They were up in arms. Why hadn't the beaver been "humanely" treated? Why hadn't it been live-trapped and relocated?

Nowhere in the article did I find anything but a systemized transferral of the blame from the newspaper-reading public to the men who actually set the trap. This was a typical case of Walt Disney biology. Simply live-trap the beaver, move it to where it will live happily ever after. But where? The beaver was already home. The truth was that the irrigation system, the hobby farms, and the suburban people had sentenced the beaver to death and the responsibility should be accepted, not pushed off on a couple of guys who we've hired to be our executioners. The death of animals displaced by human activity is the price of doing business.

That afternoon, I searched for ducks, purposely avoiding the suburb of the beaver scandal. Dolly, Jake, and Spud were all left behind; I was simply doing duck reconnaissance for the next day. I drove with the snow-capped Rocky Mountains to my right, wound my way through the foothills, then turned east until I came to scattered wheat fields. All the way I saw ducks and geese. Mostly the ducks were in the air; a few were on ponds that were not flyable. I had the feeling that, had I known the country better, I could have found plenty of good slips. But I drove a long time before I found a secluded pond with a large raft of redheads diving for food in the deepest part.

It was a perfect place. The pond itself was in a

pasture grazed short and, below the dam, a harvested wheat field rolled away for nearly a mile. There was a power line a quarter mile to the south of the pond but the wind was out of the north, so the ducks would probably fly away from the dangerous steel lines. I watched the ducks through the spotting scope. The drakes, with their bright red heads and black chests, stood out from the plain brown hens. It was impossible to get an accurate count because at any one time, several were under the water. There were at least twenty, enough for a wonderful flight. If conditions were right, we might even come out in the middle of the day and let Dolly soar. I was pleased with what I had found and headed back toward Denver. The shortest way would have been up Highway 83. But that would take me past the Parker sewage lagoon, so I went west until I came to Interstate 25, then headed north into the city.

When I arrived home, Spud was once again curled in Kris's lap. "You have a problem here," Kris said. "He's too friendly, too trusting. Someday you're going to see his picture in Safeway, staring at you from a milk carton."

"You're encouraging him."

"Maybe a little." Spud rolled his head over to look at me. He was upside down and nosed Kris's hand to pet him. It was hard to believe that this was my bird dog. They looked comfortable on the couch with the "NBC Evening News" just beginning and I couldn't help joining them.

We ate a pizza that night, my first one in six months, and watched "The Cosby Show" and "Night Court." The ten o'clock news said that snow would move in at the beginning of the week. We cleaned up the kitchen and went to bed. But I didn't go right to sleep. I lay staring into the night, and thought about the migration. Where would Dolly be if she were on her own? Far to the south by now. She would be a much better flyer, a better hunter by now if she had had parents to learn from instead of me. My right ear was close to the open window, and I thought that I heard geese in the night.

By morning it had turned cold. There was no chance of Dolly finding a thermal, so we didn't leave for the pond with the redheads until three o'clock. Spud stayed at home; Jake and I drove slowly southeast. It was after three-thirty when I looked into the spotting scope toward the pond. My mood disintegrated. The ducks were gone. Over and over I scanned the edges of the pond. But the pond was empty except for a thin layer of ice that had formed in the night. Finally I admitted that there were no ducks, and realized that our only chance for a flight was the Parker sewage lagoon.

We drove up Highway 83 and turned onto the service road. This time there was no hesitation. We parked, put Dolly up, negotiated the fence, and flushed the ducks. Dolly caught one very much as before, but this time we found her right away. I hurried her more than I should have, but I didn't want to be caught trespassing. By five-thirty Jake and I were home, the faintly pungent smell clinging to my clothes and to his fur.

For the next three days, we hit the Parker sewage lagoon around four-thirty. Dolly became deadly. She learned to wait until the ducks had cleared the chain-link fence before her stoop. The stoop forced them below the fence, making it impossible to return to the water. She stopped hitting them in the air and simply herded them into the ground where she grabbed them easily. Jake and I had become proficient too. The entire procedure took less than ten minutes.

It was not until I was at the very top of the fence for the sixth time, just swinging my leg over the barbed wire, that it occurred to me how awful this was. I hung there, eight feet off the ground, with the foul pond below me. Jake waited patiantly on the other side. Dolly circled overhead and above her boiled the gray clouds of winter. I lowered myself to the ground beside Jake who looked up as if he knew what was going through my mind. I called Dolly down to the lure and left that place.

Again that night I lay in bed thinking. My good ear was close to the window; I strained to hear the geese. After awhile Kris shook me. She was on my left and had apparently been trying to talk to me. I tilted my head toward her in the dark so that I could hear. "You'll be leaving, won't you?" I nodded and held her head tight against my chest. Then the sound of the geese came through the window. It began in the distance, the flock beginning to rise off the pond six blocks away, and increased in intensity as they came toward us. The air was filled with honking, a cacophony of migrating geese. It drowned out everything. Even my thoughts.

If a person had eyes like a peregrine they could see the Llano Estacado from the top of Raton Pass. I pulled off the highway just as the road began to fall from Colorado into New Mexico. The cedars thin out there and if the day is clear, as it almost always is, you can see thousands of square miles of northeastern New Mexico, and the panhandles of Texas and Oklahoma. Just beyond human vision is the twenty-seven-million-acre plateau that rises along the boundary of Texas and New Mexico called the Llano Estacado.

Though most historians agree that Coronado named the area Llano Estacado in 1541, there is disagreement on just what the name means. *Llano* means "plains," and *estacado* is translated as either "staked" or "stockaded," as in enclosed by upright logs or pickets. One explanation for the name suggests that the caprock escarpment on the Texas side and the Mescalero escarpment along the Pecos River in New Mexico rise up to form the Llano Estacado in such a way that Coronado was reminded of a fort and so intended the name to mean "the stockaded plains." Another explanation claims that the tall spikes of the yucca plants reminded Coronado of "stakes." But the explanation that I have always liked is that the Llano Estacado is so vast and flat, with so few natural landmarks, that Coronado's expedition was forced to carry large wooden stakes with them to drive into the ground as navigation points to insure that they would not be lost.

The Llano Estacado is one of the most unique areas in North America. Less than fifty miles from where I parked is the Folsom archeological dig; here in 1925, researchers found the remnants of an ancient mass-killing site. The bones at the site belonged to *Bison antiquus*, the much larger ancestor of the modern "American buffalo." There were no anatomical remains of hunters found at the site, although they left their mark in the form of flint artifacts. These finely crafted, fluted spear-points were 8,000 to 10,000 years old: They have become known as Folsom points. The flint to make them came from the Alibates quarries, located at the northern edge of the Llano. These quarries supplied native Americans with high-quality flint for nearly 15,000 years. There are at least nine other sites of different primitive cultures scattered around the Llano Estacado. It has always been a land of hunters and hunting cultures. The oldest of these cultures, the Clovis culture (approximately 12,000 B.C.), was apparently centered near a winter camp that is still in use. Jim Weaver and Kent Carnie have hunted on the edge of the Llano Estacado since the late 1970s. Their camp was my destination.

I drove through Raton Pass and entered New Mexico. Here the vegetation was more sparse, the cedars stunted, the yuccas grew from rock. I turned off the interstate and began our long descent into the Canadian River drainage. In the little town of Mosquero I ate green chili and tortillas and bought a New Mexico hunting license and game restoration stamp. That brought the number of permits that I had bought to nineteen. I still needed two more for Texas and the last permit, the one to release Dolly, was still being debated by the authorities. Though agencies had paid hundreds of thousands of dollars to restore endangered species, I had received a skeptical response when I suggested that I would like to release a peregrine falcon on the Texas beach for nothing.

We camped in a dry draw above the Canadian River, not far from a pond where I had seen a raft of ducks. Dolly was ready to concentrate on other game. Ducks were easy for her. She had learned about all there was to learn from flying them, and there was a danger that she would become "wedded" to them and not want to fly smaller or more difficult birds. She would have to be proficient at many kinds of game if she was to have a chance on her own. This would be the last duck that Jake and I would help her catch.

It was nearly the first of December. Though the mountains, the northern plains, and the grasslands were dead for the winter, the weather here on Llano Estacado was like autumn. The early afternoon was warm and clear, and as I removed Dolly's hood, it occurred to me that she might soar. And soar she did. Jake and I stood watching as she searched for a thermal along the dry ridges that formed the northern boundary of the Canadian River bottom. When she found one, she set her wings and did not flap again until she was out of sight. I could still see her in the binoculars when we started for the pond. But by the time we were in position to flush the ducks from the pond, I had lost her. I hoped she was still above me and told Jake to go ahead.

Near the pond there was a single telephone wire stretched between several poles. The line ran through an area of bluestem grass fifty yards from the pond. Though it was dangerous, I felt sure the ducks would be far past it before Dolly caught up to them. Jake launched into the air and the ducks, which I recognized as lesser scaup, ran across the water and rose in one mass. I didn't hear the rumbling rush of air through Dolly's wings until they were far past the telephone wire. But lesser scaup are not strong flyers, and when they heard the stoop they turned quickly inside of Dolly. She was going too fast to adjust to that change in direction. But at the bottom of her stoop, she set her wings and rode the arc of an inside loop to a pitch several hundred feet above the flock. Now she commanded them easily and although they headed back toward the pond, there was no chance for them to escape. She reached them just as they crossed the field of bluestem, before they came to the telephone line, and drove through them, coming out the other side with a lesser scaup secure in her talons. It was all too fast for me to tell what happened, but the power of that second stoop clearly intimidated the flock, and many of the scaup crashed into the field of bluestem.

Dolly settled onto a small knoll not far from the pond. Jake and I sat beside her as she ate. The scaup was a hen with very plain feathers. The only hint of flamboyance was the bright eye and the light ring of feathers around the beak. I picked up the head that Dolly had severed and buried it at the base of a yucca. Jake lay down but quickly raised his head and sniffed the air. I could see that he wanted to explore the smell, so I told him it was all right. He ambled off toward the field of bluestem.

I was watching Dolly when I heard Jake behind me. His tail wagged in the dry grass and Dolly flattened her feathers and craned her neck to look at him. I turned and there sat Jake with another scaup in his mouth. I quickly moved between him and Dolly, who had altered her stance to fly at Jake and take the duck away. Jake happily gave me the duck unhurt, stood up, and trotted off. I tucked the duck under my coat so Dolly could not see it and moved toward the pond. When I eased the scaup into the water it dove and was gone. It probably swam underwater to the reeds at the other end of the pond. There it would hide until we were gone. I chuckled to myself as I walked back to Dolly. But to Jake, this was no joke. In two minutes he was back with another duck. Apparently they had been so frightened by Dolly's stoop that they have not moved from where they had crashed into the grass near the telephone line.

Jake worked steadily for the next twenty minutes. He brought back six healthy lesser scaup that had decided they would rather be picked up by this huge black dog than fly and risk drawing another stoop from Dolly. Instinct had driven them into the ground, an evasive tactic that had evolved naturally. Countless lesser scaup have escaped falcon stoops by flying to the ground.

I deposited all six ducks in the pond. Then Jake retrieved one that was dead. Its left wing, and the breast muscle that powered it, were torn away from the body, and the neck was broken. I held the twisted mess in my hand and knew immediately what had happened. This duck had been going full speed, perhaps heading for the grass like the others, when it encountered something that the species had not had time to evolve a resistance to. The duck had flown full force into the telephone line and been torn nearly in half. I had seen it before. Wires were a leading killer and disabler of birds. The damage that had been done to the lesser scaup was amazing. It gave me a chill to think that Dolly had flown very close to that same wire, at perhaps twice the speed.

※

The next day we made our way along the western edge of the Llano Estacado. We moved along narrow back roads that made no more mark on the landscape than a pencil line on a painting. The Llano is unbelievably flat. It was easy to imagine the trouble that Coronado had experienced during his insane odyssey in search of nonexistent golden cities. The vegetation was all the same then. It must have been easy to become lost. And as I traveled, the image of those armor-suited Spaniards—sweating and out of place like Custer's troops in Montana—moved through my mind. They had come here in 1540, the soldiers looking for gold and the friars looking for their own kind of treasure, in the form of converts. I wished that I had seen them out here, clattering along with all the trappings of Europe, carrying those heavy wooden stakes that they planned to drive into the Llano to insure that they would not be swallowed by the landscape. I wondered what went through the mind of the Turk, the Indian who guided the expedition.

Great sections of the Llano are now under plow, although it is one of the best examples of an area that should never be plowed. The fertile sandy soil, once torn by the plow, drifted wherever the wind blew it: over the roads, on top of the buildings and fences, until it would gather into huge piles or dunes, usually at the ends of the fields. What had once been a lush grassland where buffalo grazed by the tens of thousands was now a virtual desert, a patchwork of "blown-out" farming ventures.

For one reason or another, this land only makes a crop once every three years. It is quite possible that more tons of hay, more pounds of red meat, were produced on the Llano before the white man came. Perhaps the Turk sensed that. Perhaps that is why he purposely led the Spaniards out onto the Llano, farther and farther from the gentle farmers of the New Mexican pueblos, in the hope that they would be lost forever. The Turk was summarily strangled to death when Coronado learned what he had done. He had led the Spaniards away from the New Mexican pueblos for months, deeper into the Llano Estacado and closer and closer to certain and horrible death. Another brave, forgotten hero.

And still it goes on. Justified by the first page of the Bible that clearly says that man is superior to all that surrounds him, men have come onto the Llano with God's own command to "subdue" it. Driven by a belief that the earth was created for their consumption, they have done battle with nature. As I drove across the Llano that day, it was clear that man was losing. Nature had suffered too, through erosion from wind and water, and the loss of native plants through overgrazing. But the men looked the worse for the battle. This is a land of poor, hollow-faced people. They stood staring from the street corners in the dying little towns with an odd, comic look on their faces. That look reminded me of a cartoon. It was the look of Sylvester the Cat after finding out, the hard way, that the box he thought held a mouse actually held a kangaroo.

Because the Llano Estacado is so delicate, man's

abuses are more apparent than in other areas. It is clear
that the Llano is turning into a desert because of plowing. But for a while yet, the Llano is still a wonderful,
wild place. Ducks, geese, and cranes winter here, flock-
ing around the playas that have not been permanently
drained for farming. There are antelope and deer.
Scaled quail dart between the yuccas, and incredible
numbers of lesser prairie chickens roam the plains. But
perhaps best of all, the weedy grain fields and abandoned farms provide homes for covey after covey of
bobwhite quail. The night before, I had heard their
familiar bob-bob-white call and I brought out my old
twenty-gauge. As I rubbed the shotgun with an oily rag,
I was reminded of the morning twenty years ago when I
sat in the thin morning light of an Ohio dawn with that
gun. I was only a boy that morning, but old enough to
be called for a draft physical, old enough to know I was
threatened. As I rubbed the maple stock in the lantern's
yellow light, I felt as if I was back in Ohio. Finally I
lowered my head and pressed my left ear against the
middle of the long barrels. I pulled the triggers, but this
time there were no shells in the chambers.

The next day, when we came to a likely abandoned farm, I pulled into the overgrown driveway and
let Spud out for his first quail hunt. Now it was warm so
I let Jake out, but tied him to the truck so that I could
direct all my attention toward Spud. Both dogs picked
up my excitement, but Jake realized that this was not his
day to hunt. He breathed heavily and wagged his tail
but did not strain on the rope. Spud was crazy. He leapt
into the air, turning nearly a hundred and eighty de-
grees before coming down. He ran back and forth as I

pulled my hunting coat out of the truck. Finally he sat and barked at me. When I told him to "go on," he exploded into a flat-out gallop down the driveway.

The bobwhite quail is a small, round bird not much larger than a meadowlark, and to the uninitiated it might not seem like much when compared to a pheasant or a grouse. But the bobwhite sets the standard for durability, courage, workability for a dog, and odd as it may sound, manners. They are gentle birds who pair up, one cock to one hen and, if successful, raise twelve to fifteen chicks a year. Once grown, they gather together in single family or multiple family groups called coveys. Their bodies pressed tightly together create more warmth, and with more eyes they are safer from predators. The fact that bobwhites are found in coveys is one of the things that make them a joy to hunt. A covey rising in front of a pointed dog is a thrill, and working the singles after they have scattered tests the best of dogs.

Spud was not the best of dogs, but he had potential. He had begun to find, point, and handle birds, and had shown some real signs that he might make a retriever. I had great hopes that quail would hone his abilities and give me a chance to correct some of his faults.

The farmstead I had found was an ideal place for bobwhites. Its six tumbled-down buildings were surrounded by a poor grove of trees with a weedy sorghum field beyond. There were twisted pieces of machinery tangled in the underbrush and a corral filled with tumbleweeds. I walked the driveway after Spud, and when he circled past, I called him in and made him sit and calm down. He was used to open prairie where the birds were few and the distances great. There were probably more birds in this thirty acres than there had been in three hundred acres farther north. I tried to explain this to Spud, but he only sat shaking and panting like a lunatic. I sent him on but kept talking to him to slow him down.

We worked the edge of the corral and I saw quail tracks in the dust. Then we swung out through the old tree grove, and Spud began to get birdy. He lowered into a crouch, and his tail whipped double-time as he moved into the light breeze. I trotted to catch up, as he flash-pointed and moved on. The covey was ahead of him, but he was not sure exactly where. He firmed up again, but a tiny twitch of his tail told me that he did not have them pinpointed. I didn't want him to get too close and flush them, so I slid two shells into the gun, told Spud to "whoa," and moved ahead of him. I watched him over my shoulder and talked to him. He stared intently into the grass and became even more rigid. Then the covey exploded at my feet.

I tried to be calm, to pick out a quail that had gotten up early, then one of the late risers. Instead, I spun quickly, twisting my feet in the grass and nearly fell. I screamed "stop" at Spud, who charged past me, then I fired twice into the air. At times like that I am thankful that my shotgun only holds two shells. Had it held four, or five, or fifteen shells, the outcome would have been the same: lots of noise, no quail, and an empty gun. Spud took off, chasing the quail. But of course he couldn't catch one; only a puppy would think he could. He came back in ten minutes with his sides heaving like a blacksmith's bellows. I would have disciplined him for chasing the birds, but it wouldn't be fair. No one was there to discipline me.

We sat in the shade of one of the dwarfed trees until we both cooled down. Waiting served several purposes, not the least of which was to give the quail a chance to put down enough scent so that Spud could smell them. Unlike a covey, a single gives off little scent and can be easy to miss. We waited for twenty minutes, and I promised myself that if something good happened, we would stop for the day, giving Spud a solid foundation for the next lesson.

We walked toward the quail, and I kept Spud close. He quartered in front of me and we worked through the rest of the trees and out into the weedy sorghum field. It had been a covey of probably twenty birds and I felt sure that we would come across a few of them. Spud had shown that he had a pretty good nose in Nebraska. If he could find bobwhite singles I would be pleased.

We made a sweep into the sorghum. Twice I thought that I heard the wurlee-he of a single calling for the rest of the covey. The call seemed to come from far out in the sorghum, so I was surprised when Spud froze not six feet in front of me. But he had already gotten too close and the quail sprang into the air. I did not even try to shoot but immediately shouted "whoa." Spud had started to go after the quail, but I was right there and he stopped, looking after it like it was a lover leaving on a train. I got my hands on him and stroked his sides. "Good boy."

When I sent him on, he started in the direction

the quail had gone. "Leave it!" I shouted, and he turned and hunted in front of me. He hadn't gone more than fifty feet when he snapped onto a point. This time he looked like he knew what he was doing, rock solid, tail arched over his back. "Easy," I said, folding two shells into the gun. "Easy." I touched him before I moved ahead. When the bird came up, I shot, and told Spud to fetch it.

Spud crashed through the sorghum so fast that he overran the dead bird. But he had smelled it. He turned in midair, and I could hear his nose sniffing through the dry sorghum leaves like an Electrolux. When he found the bird, he made a quick, violent move, but when he brought it to my hand, I saw he had not even punctured the skin. He was so happy, he wiggled all over and whined with joy. I patted him on the head and gave myself a mental slap on the back. Then I heard the wurlee-he call again out in the sorghum. But I resisted. I kept my promise, took Spud by the collar, and retraced our steps out of the field.

It was dark by the time I got to their camp, but neither Jim nor Kent had returned from flying their falcons. I let the dogs out and weighed Dolly. She had eaten a good meal the day before but nothing since. A fat peregrine can go for days without eating before it begins to lose strength. I tried to keep Dolly at a good flying weight by feeding her the equivalent of about one quail per day. That night she weighed twenty-eight and a half ounces, a good weight to begin her most difficult trial yet: late season lesser prairie chickens. I fed the dogs and unrolled my sleeping bag beside Jim's Airstream trailer. Then I walked the truck ruts out toward the north, the direction Jim would probably return from.

It was dry, clear, and cooling fast. The moon was coming up huge and orange, refracting its light through tons of invisible Texas dust. I could have been the only human for fifty miles, but I wasn't lonely. I felt perfectly at home without another person for many miles. I was walking back to the empty camp, when headlights appeared in the west. On the Llano Estacado electric lights can be seen for many, many miles. It is one of the only places that I know where, if you are lost, it might be a bad idea to walk toward a farm light. You might be walking for thirty miles. So it was a long time before Jim's pickup caught up with me. I stood in the wheel ruts with my thumb thrust out while he bounced slowly across the field. In the beam of his headlights, kangaroo mice leapt and scurried around the bunch grass. Dan and Lucky, Jim's two hunting dogs, stood in the back of the pickup. Inside, Jim sat behind the wheel with Seeker, his hybrid gyrfalcon/peregrine on his right fist. "I wondered if you were going to show up this week," he said. After I shut my door, he reached across and shifted the pickup into gear with his left hand.

We ate medium-rare prairie chicken with onions, green peppers, and tortillas. It is one of the finest meals on earth. We drank Bailey's Irish Cream liqueur and soda because it is the closest thing to chocolate malts you can make without ice cream. And we talked—about politics, books, the environment, movies, women, bird dogs, falcons, music, old friends, horses, and the ice cream that we didn't have. Kent Carnie, whose trailer was parked nearby, had gone into Lubbock, Texas, for the night. The Bailey's was gone, and it was long after midnight when we decided that it was time to go to bed. We had played all Jim's tapes by then and had come to the one he always plays when I visit. He calls it his tape of dead dog songs. The last thing we did before I went out into the cool, clear Llano night to find my sleeping bag was to sit quietly listening to "Old Bugler" and "Queen of the Rails."

When I finally crawled into my sleeping bag and looked up at the sky I felt very lucky. There were no skies like that in Ohio and I was thankful that I had failed that military physical all those years ago. In a strange way, I realized I had been exiled to this. The sky above me was the same one that shone over my home in South Dakota. If the air quality was good in Denver, Kris might be staring up at the very same stars. Thousands of coyotes, owls, and rodents were glancing upward just then. Perhaps somewhere, on a cottonwood snag above a prairie river, or on the lee-side of a sand dune on the Llano Estacado, a wild peregrine falcon had just stirred from its sleep and brought its head out from under its wing to gaze at the sky. I imagined those eyes, those different ways of seeing, sending lines of vision upward from the great plains. I imagined all those lines mingling in the air above me until they were indistinguishable, the same vision. When I finally closed my eyes, I slid my hand under my sleeping pad and found, for the first time in months, that I had forgotten to put the pistol under it. I slept soundly, and dreamed of Dolly riding the wild, salty air of Padre Island.

Kent returned in the morning so Jim and I left Dolly and Seeker blocked out in his care while we went quail hunting. We took the two puppies, Spud and Lucky, and left Dan, Jim's old setter, at home to rest for the more important work of pointing prairie chickens that afternoon. Prairie chickens are much more difficult to point properly and Dan was the only dog with the experience to handle them. Gun hunting for quail was a training ground for pointing prairie chickens and grouse under falcons.

The puppies did well. We shot enough for a noon snack and a few to put in Jim's smoker. Back at the camp we gobbled the delicate white meat while the falcons dozed in the sun after their baths. I was tense because this would be Dolly's introduction to lesser prairie chickens, which are really grouse. They are the southern version of the sharp-tailed grouse. They are extremely difficult to catch for any falcon, but particularly for a small peregrine. Though Dolly had caught many ducks, pheasants, and partridge, grouse were different. She had been flown only at one and, though she caught it, it had been a fluke. She was a competent hunter but would be lucky indeed to kill a prairie chicken this late in the season.

Because a good dog is essential to a classic flight at any grouse, I was glad when Jim offered to take me out with him. The prairie chicken population is subject to radical fluctuations. Weather conditions and land usage can have tremendous effects on the number of chickens that hatch and survive. Some years there are plenty of chickens, some years it is hard to find one. That year there were enough, but I was told you had to hunt for them.

So we set out from camp with our falcons on our fists and Dan casting magnificent, two-hundred-yard sweeps through the grass and shin oak in front of us. There are many kinds of hunters. There are those whose real interest is in shooting. There are those who like to watch the falcons fly. And there are those who, as Ortega y Gasset points out, have chosen not to be spectators of nature but rather participants. They are people who allow the quarry to be more than an abstract notion of a deer, or a rabbit, or a grouse; people who go to great lengths to find the essence of the game they seek and who, once they find it, recognize that essence and respect it. Jim Weaver is that kind of hunter. As we walked out from camp, he checked the wind, noted the temperature, observed hundreds of signs, and called on decades of experience. When we didn't find chickens where we thought we should, he rethought and backtracked. We watched the harriers, hoping they would lead us to the chickens. We walked miles out of our way so that Dan would be working into the wind when we came to the most likely places. We kept our eyes open, walked, and searched. But we found no chickens.

That is when Jim, like any true hunter, invoked his muse. He stopped in the center of a huge pasture of shin oak and, hindered slightly by Seeker on his right fist, raised his arms. "Okay, God. We've walked a good ten miles. You mean to tell me that there aren't any chickens out here?" Dan had stopped running and was lying down. He had apparently heard this speech before. "We don't ask for much. We need two chickens. Two measly chickens. Nothing to you, the world to us. I always thank you for them. You know I'll thank you this time." He lowered his arms, then thrust his free hand into the air again and held up two fingers. "Two chickens. That's all we ask."

I had been standing thirty feet away during Jim's speech and when it was over, started to walk toward him. I had not taken two steps when a pair of prairie chickens flushed at my feet. They cackled off in their twisting, mocking flight and we both watched them until they landed. One was a hundred yards away and the other twice that far.

Dolly was given the first slip. She left my fist quickly and flew strongly into a five-mile-per-hour wind. Jim had marked the first chicken down with reference to two fence posts and now worked Dan in on it. Dolly continued to mount into the wind. She had learned from ducks that her best chance was to wait on upwind so that the force of the wind would be added to the force of her stoop. She flew with her regular confidence. She had not failed to kill for weeks, but she had not flown prairie chickens and Jim and I both knew she was about to get a lesson. Dan locked onto point. I swung upwind, hoping to get the chicken to flush downwind.

By the time I was ready to flush, Dolly was in a good position. I walked right at Dan's nose and when the chicken came up it flew right past him. It cackled and twisted as it went.

Dolly's stoop was nearly vertical. She expected to overtake the chicken like she overtook ducks. But she did not fly through it like she usually did. She did make contact, but only with a wing, as the chicken did a complete barrel roll to evade her grasp. She pitched up, expecting the chicken to give up and crash into the ground. But the chicken was just getting started. After the roll, it changed directions and flew into the wind where its short, powerful wings gave it a clear advantage. Dolly's second stoop was weak in comparison, and she ended up flapping ineffectually far behind the disappearing prairie chicken.

It was about what I had expected. Grouse were perhaps too tough for Dolly at this stage, and although we would try again, I knew that she would probably never be called upon to kill one after she was free. Her life would depend on her ability to catch smaller birds. I swung the lure and she came in. It had been a long time since she had not killed. After I had picked her up and hooded her, I moved behind Jim as he unhooded Seeker and sent Dan to pinpoint the second chicken.

Though most people would be hard-pressed to tell Dolly and Seeker apart, they were very different falcons. The gyrfalcon's shorter wings were apparent and beat quicker and stronger than a peregrine's. Seeker had killed hundreds of prairie chickens and he knew exactly what to do. He pumped straight into the wind over Dan's point until he was three hundred feet high. He did not set his wings but continued to pump them as he watched Jim over his shoulder.

When the prairie chicken flushed he flipped backward and pumped his wings double-time for the first two hundred feet of the stoop. As a result, the chicken had no time for the fancy maneuver that had distracted Dolly. Seeker hit the chicken hard enough for me to hear the whack clearly a hundred yards away. The chicken wobbled, fell ten feet, but regained control and rocketed ahead. Seeker had anticipated this and had already positioned himself for a second stoop. The chicken realized that this was no rookie peregrine, and headed for cover. Seeker seemed to know where it was going and they sprinted toward an overgrown sand dune on the horizon. They were almost out of sight when, in my binoculars, I saw Seeker close the gap and hit the chicken again just as they got to the dune.

It was a three-quarter mile walk and Jim had to get his telemetry receiver out to find him. We sat silently in the sand for five minutes watching Seeker eat grouse before Jim stood up. "Well," he said, "you gotta promise you won't tell anybody about this." I nodded my head. "I can't believe how often that works," he said sinking to his knees. "Thank you," he said. He was talking to God again, but I noticed that Jim held two handfuls of soil and directed his voice downward, as if he were talking to the earth itself.

When we got back to camp, Mack Kizer was there. He is the owner of the land where we camp and hunt. Mack is a farmer and a good one. He refuses to do anything to his land that might hurt it. Mack's father was a farmer, and now he has four boys of his own. But his land and his life are under siege.

We talked that night of the neighbor (actually he lives in town and is a businessman) who has plowed the land next to Mack's to qualify for a government program even though he knows it will never grow a crop. The loose soil had blown onto Mack's land and completely covered his fence. We agreed that this was a crime against us all, yet it was condoned and encouraged by government policy. It was subsidized desertification, a problem so horrendous that we fell silent.

But by then the prairie chicken and quail were sizzling with the onions. Jim had made corn bread in a dutch oven and Kent had brought fresh broccoli from Lubbock. We convinced Mack to stay for dinner and got him talking about his boys. Right then their main interest was basketball, but Mack told us that the oldest had begun to notice girls. "In fact," Mack said in his shy way, "he's goin' out girlin' Friday night." Mack said this with pride and obvious concern. What Mack had communicated was that soon there would be another generation, another set of young families on this land. He was proud about that. But the concern in his voice reflected his worry about what would become of the next generation. He wondered if there was any way they too could be farmers. He wondered if his sons would be able to stay on the land.

❧

Every day for the next week, we hunted quail and Spud became steadily more proficient. Every afternoon Dolly flew at prairie chickens. She was flying harder and harder, staying up for an hour at a time and pursuing the chickens great distances. She pounded them, repeatedly knocked feathers loose and drove them into the ground. But she did not catch one. Two days before I planned to leave for Padre Island, we found a group of a hundred prairie chickens in a sorghum field. She knocked down six, one after the other, from great heights, but every one got up and flew to safety before she could grasp it on the ground.

Even though I was discouraged, she continued to fly hard. I did not feed her the day before our last try. She was as hungry as she could get before she would start to lose strength. It was a condition she might find herself in many times when she was wild; or a condition she would find herself in only once. That last evening was a sort of dress rehearsal for the day when she would not have me and the lure as a safety net.

I drove back to the field where we had found the huge flock and, although it was an inferior way to hunt, sat at the edge of the sorghum and waited for them to come in to feed. While I waited, alert for any sign of movement in the air, meadowlarks flew in and out of the field, a coyote hunted mice on the opposite edge of the sorghum, ferruginous hawks sat on power poles in the distance and harriers worked the flat lands in search of small birds and rodents. It was a wonderfully clear late afternoon and everything seemed to be out feeding or playing in the last warmth of the day.

As the sun went lower the temperature cooled, and I began to think that the prairie chickens were not coming that night. I had almost decided to give up, drive back to camp, feed Dolly, and get ready for the long haul to Padre Island, when an eerie hush fell over me. It was as if I had lost hearing in my other ear, like the barometric pressure had suddenly dropped. Before I was aware of what was happening, the lack of sound had become a whir. Then it was the whistle of a hun-

dred pairs of wings and the entire flock of prairie chickens flew right over my head. A few cackled and twisted
and I heard Dolly's bells in the back of the truck.

They settled into the sorghum a hundred yards
out. I marked them down and watched for a while with
my binoculars. A few chickens leapt into the air in mock
battle, a few pecked at the fallen sorghum, and some
simply rested between the rows. I got Dolly ready to fly.
Then, using the truck to shield her from the chickens, I
unhooded her. Though I wasn't watching her, I knew
when Dolly was about to spread her wings to fly. If you
concentrate, you can feel a peregrine become lighter just
before she leaves your fist. It is their anticipation of
flight, their mind-set that does it. If you don't watch
them take off, if you just feel it, you would swear that
they blend with the air somehow, simply become
lighter, until finally gravity is not an obstacle.

Dolly left the fist as if she had disappeared, but in
the binoculars I saw that she was still very real to the
prairie chickens who squatted down when they saw
her. I lined up on a mesquite tree so that I would be able
to go straight to the chickens. I began to walk slowly
toward them. And Dolly flew stronger than she had
ever flown. That day she was as hungry as she had ever
been. She flew like a wild falcon, as if her life depended
on it.

Dolly made two large circles to gain altitude, then
tightened the circles and remained just over my right
shoulder as I walked toward the chickens. The circles
became very small, but she continued to gain altitude
and did not set her wings. I watched her and she
watched just ahead of me. Then a chicken flushed far to

my left, and she tipped but did not stoop. She had learned that she didn't have a chance unless the flush was perfect. I took another step and up came two more chickens. She had begun her stoop when the entire flock rose around me.

The air was filled with the cackle and whir of prairie chickens. They were everywhere, going in all directions, but one in particular stood out to me, and I knew that this was the one Dolly had chosen. Everything else fell away, there was no more noise, no more flashing wings, the wind went dead. I stood still beneath two converging vectors. It seemed to take a long time and neither the straight line of the prairie chicken nor the soft-bellied curve of the plummeting peregrine seemed to move fast. It was not until the prairie chicken exploded in a burst of feathers that I understood the force of the collision.

The prairie chicken never flapped its wings again but hit the ground, bouncing three feet before it rolled to a stop. Dolly pitched up and settled down. But this time there was no doubt in my mind that the prairie chicken would stay put. It had clearly been killed in the stoop. When Dolly grasped its head it only quivered, then lay still. A light shower of down drifted on the gentle breeze. It floated into the sorghum stubble and tiny, fluffy pieces settled into my hair.

When I described the flight that night, Jim knew just what I had seen. We were silent for a long time. "She'll never be more ready to go against it," he said. And I knew that he meant she was as close to a wild peregrine as I could make her. And we both knew that her chances for survival were poor. There were so many

things that could go wrong. It was a wonder that anything survived in our world. We both knew that from
our experience hacking young peregrines. So what did I
think I was doing? Was I just another silly human with
an anthropocentric view of the world?

LAGUNA
MADRE

We didn't leave camp until late afternoon. Originally, I had planned to drive all night because I wanted to get Dolly to the coast as soon as possible. But around 5 A.M., just as the sky began to brighten to the east, I was overcome by exhaustion. I pulled off the road, resolving to rest for an hour or so. As soon as I fell asleep, the dream came: Padre Island, all the birds and grasses and shrubs. Salt spray on my lips, the steady wash of surf and Dolly on my fist. Her jesses were cut away, and she stared out over the Gulf of Mexico with black eyes that did not acknowledge my presence. The pintail drake was there, waiting on the pond, just over the rise and out of my sight.

She caught the sea breeze and banked away from me over the sand dunes. Then she found a thermal and set her wings and rode it up. In my dream I could still see her clearly. But again I did not see the stoop. I flushed the drake and turned away, walking slowly to the pickup where the dogs waited for me to take them home.

I awoke, still tired, with the thought of that long trip north still in my head. By ten o'clock, however, I was ready to fly Dolly. It had rained heavily on the countryside outside of San Antonio and the flooded fields were thick with killdeer and snipe. I put Dolly up half a mile away and let her fly. She powered into the light breeze, and because it was early and she was not hungry, she played in the air. I lay on the hood of the pickup and watched her. She made a long, flat, playful stoop at the killdeer on the edge of a field. Even from half a mile away, I could hear them shriek. But Dolly was not serious.

Finally she drifted north and found a thermal that topped out at perhaps a thousand feet. Then she broke away and flew toward a puddle where several killdeer and snipe stood motionless. I walked slowly along the road just under Dolly, then climbed the fence and ran toward the water. The killdeer and snipe flushed like bats. Dolly corkscrewed downward, neatly plucking a snipe from the air. She set her wings and glided a hundred yards with the snipe tucked in her talons. She landed on a small dry knoll and I let her eat the whole snipe before I picked her up and got back into the pickup to drive toward San Antonio.

My plan was to check into a motel and get a good night's sleep. So I drove into the city and, though I didn't want to be downtown, I missed a turn and found myself surrounded by traffic. Then I saw the San Antonio River snaking among the tall buildings, and knew that it would lead me to the outskirts of town. But first, of course, it took me to the Alamo.

Like everyone else, I had heard about the Alamo. I had seen Fess Parker play Davy Crockett. And like many others I had thought the whole thing seemed hokey and melodramatic. But I had never seen the building itself. As soon as it came into sight—small and out of place—I knew that I had to stop. I turned my head as I passed and wandered into the next lane of traffic. A Mexican American blasted me with his horn. His Spanish, through my open window, jarred me, and I nearly turned the wrong way on a one-way street. Then, miraculously, I spotted a motel. I pulled in and took a room. I needed the sleep and this motel was a neat two blocks from the Alamo.

After I made sure that Dolly, Spud, and Jake were content in the back of the pickup, I walked to the Alamo. Though I still believed that it was a tourist trap, I walked inside and read about the history of the old mission and the siege that had made it famous. At first it was all very familiar: One hundred eighty-two men died there in the name of Texas independence. It seemed, at first, to be just another patriotic war memorial. But there was more. I learned that couriers came and went to the very end. One man, Bonham, carried the last communication from the outside. The message said simply that there would be no help coming. Bonham delivered the message and stayed to face inevitable death. The truth was that they all could have left anytime they pleased, but chose to stay. Thirty-two men actually fought their way *into* the besieged fort at the eleventh hour to die. They rode hard from the town of Gonzales to get there before Santa Ana sealed off the fort.

As I walked over the two-hundred-year-old stone floor, reading one bronze placard after another, it became apparent to me that this was a memorial to a different kind of war than I was used to. There were no draftees or dissenters at the Alamo. Many were not even Texans; they were from Tennessee, Kentucky, Ohio, New York, England, Germany, Ireland, from everywhere and nowhere. Most had not been in Texas for more than a few months. As I read, I learned that they had died without even knowing that Texas had declared independence. The flag of Mexico had been flown by both the attackers and the defenders at the Alamo.

I could detect no political or economic reason for what seemed, ostensibly, to be an act of collective insanity. I read the pieces of the defenders' histories displayed on those old stone walls. They were frontiersmen and adventurers who, perhaps for the first time, had found something that they agreed on. The placards claimed that they had died for the glory of Texas. I doubted it. When I walked out of the Alamo and into the San Antonio afternoon, it seemed more likely that those one hundred eighty-two men died because they couldn't adjust to a changing environment. The Alamo was an excuse.

My visit to the Alamo left me even more exhausted than before, but I walked the streets of San Antonio until it was dark. Then I found the river again and walked along it, past the shops and restaurants, and heard Spanish music drifting from the bars. I ate enchiladas on the sidewalk and watched the ladies in white dresses pass on the arms of dark gentlemen. Then fatigue overtook me, and I returned to the motel. For some reason I brought Dolly, Spud, and Jake into the room with me and went to bed.

But my sleep was fitful and at three o'clock I was wide awake. For some reason, I thought about the morning I had held my left ear to the side of the shotgun and pulled both triggers. In the dark I imagined how the blast tore the nerves of the cochlea and left it unrepairable. I lay in the dark and felt a light sweat form on my forehead. Then I felt a dog jump softly onto the bed and lie down gently against my side. I reached out and touched Jake's big old head. It was soft and strong and, just then, was the most comforting thing I could imagine.

But sleep did not return, and by five o'clock I was driving again, down Interstate 37 toward Corpus Christi and Padre Island. At Pleasanton, I turned off the Interstate and headed straight south toward Freer. Somewhere in the middle of McMullen county, I found a gravel road heading east into tangled cactus country. I saw small Texas white-tailed deer, and once I thought I caught sight of a javelina or wild hog as it retreated from the road into the thorny bushes of the barrow ditch.

I drove for almost an hour along that road before I found what I was looking for. A mud track led off to the left and I could see some deserted buildings a quarter mile north. This was probably someone's private quail hunting spot, so I hid the pickup behind an old granary. There are terrible stories about what happens to Texas quail poachers, but this would be Spud's last chance of the year, and it was too early for most people to be out checking on their land. Besides, though I had complied with countless rules in the last months, I had already decided to release Dolly with or without a permit. Once I had made that decision another broken law seemed a trivial thing. In fact, it felt good.

I pieced the double barrel together and let the dogs out. Jake trotted behind Spud but returned to heel. Spud cast out along a weedy bean field and turned into the wind to follow a line of trees. He zigzagged from one clump of cover to another. He leapt high in the air occasionally so he could see over the thick undergrowth. He seemed to stay in the air a long time on these leaps, and his black and white ears flapped as if he were flying. When he crossed the path in front of me, he turned into the wind and suddenly tensed. Then he moved ahead cautiously and froze.

He was staunch for the covey rise, and I killed two. I sent the dogs to retrieve and then on ahead to find more. We located three singles and I dropped them. There was another covey under an old combine and another along the edge of the bean field. Spud pointed them all and Jake retrieved and I shot until I was out of shells. When we got back to the pickup, the dogs' tongues hung out and their chests heaved. We drove to Freer and then turned east toward Alice.

It was nearly dark when I reached Corpus Christi. The city had changed but the causeway on the east, where Padre Island Drive crosses Laguna Madre and the Intercoastal Waterway, was as I remembered. On the far side of the causeway lies Padre Island National Seashore. I planned to camp there, behind the dunes, as close to Laguna Madre as I could get and still be in sight of the ocean. In the morning I would search for the pond and the drake pintail that I had dreamed of. Because it was a national seashore, hunting was, of course, prohibited, even with a falcon whose cousins hunted the island by the hundreds and used it as a staging area before launching across the Gulf of Mexico. If I was to fly Dolly on the national seashore, I would have to plan it well; first find the pond I was looking for and then fly her early the next day before people were up and about.

I found my camp, my last of the trip, just as the lights of the ocean-going ships started to show on the sea's horizon. I set up my tent and gathered driftwood for a fire, as the dogs raced up and down the beach. I tried to remember exactly where I had seen that first peregrine stoop through the flock of sanderlings. I could picture her in my mind. I could almost see the stretch of beach she had flown over, but I could not remember exactly where it had been. The only thing still clear after all those years was the falcon herself and the feeling that she gave to me.

I sat in front of the fire, roasting quail, as the dogs slept in the sand, and tried to retrace the steps of our migration. Instead, the image of a particular granite pinnacle continued to come to mind. It was the pinnacle near the headwaters of Adobe Creek in the San Isabel National Forest in southern Colorado, which was probably a historic peregrine nesting site. A friend and I had hiked in to prepare the pinnacle for a hack box to be helicoptered up the next day. My friend had recently been married. He and his wife had bought a house and that was all he could talk about. Slinging the box onto the pinnacle was our last job of the summer and he was anxious to get back to his wife and home.

We had hiked along Adobe Creek and reached the bottom of the pinnacle just as the sun came through some clouds. It was an easy, forty-foot climb to the top, a climb like we had done together a hundred times. I joked as I started up, and never considered using a rope though I carried one in my pack.

The top of the pinnacle was relatively flat and as soon as I got to it, I began wandering around looking for the best place to put the hack box. I was occupied with figuring out just which direction the prevailing winds might come from and where the box could best be seen by the attendants, so I didn't notice for a long time that my friend was not behind me. When I realized that he hadn't yet made the top, I went back to the edge and looked down. He leaned into the rock on a ledge not ten feet below, clinging to a crack as if his life depended on it. My first impression was that he was joking. He only needed to step up to the next ledge and scramble to the top. But when he looked up, I could see that this was no joke. His face was white and he made a feeble attempt to smile. But the smile would not come. He was trying hard to gather courage to come up.

"You need a rope?" I asked.

He tried the smile again and, probably thinking that it might seem ridiculous to me, shook his head. But I could see his knees trembling. "I'll throw you a rope," I said. "Don't be nuts."

Then he agreed, and seconds later sat on a rock on the top of the pinnacle. "I don't know what happened," he said. "I just froze."

I tried to laugh it off. "Happens to everybody," I said.

"Not on a cakewalk like that," he said. "I just don't know what happened. I was climbing along like always and then I started thinking about the new house.

I started thinking that if I fell I'd never see it again."

What he said wasn't really true. We had not been high enough to get killed. But looking down at him, pale-faced and shaking, I could see that for the first time he had realized that he had something to lose. He avoided my eyes as if he were afraid I thought less of him, so I looked away. He sat there alone, feeling bad, embarrassed, ashamed that he had frozen with fear. And there I was, looking out over a million miles of nothing, the wind strong in my face, feeling suddenly bad because I hadn't.

Sitting on the Texas beach, staring out to the ocean, I thought about the little ranch in South Dakota and about Kris. She had asked me once what I was looking for. I had mumbled a reply that probably didn't satisfy her. But she never called me on it; she knew I didn't have a good answer. Then I looked around my little camp; the dogs sleeping peacefully, quail cooking over a fire, and the sea beyond. This was part of the answer, I was sure. But only part.

I woke after a good night's sleep and blocked Dolly in the salty air as the sun rose from the ocean. Today I planned to scout the mud flats where the tourists and park rangers seldom went. After I found the right place, I would take Dolly back across the causeway to the mainland and fly her once more at snipe. That night I would come back to camp and prepare to fly her for the last time, early the next morning, at the duck that I hoped I would find today.

More quail sizzled in the skillet as Dolly took her

bath. After Dolly was dry, we all loaded into the truck and drove down the beach to a place where I could pull the pickup between sand dunes. I locked up because this was a high-traffic area, and with binoculars and a water bottle I started across the sand toward a more remote area where some sort of dredging operation had left ponds and channels that might harbor the pintail I had seen in my dreams.

Impossible as it seemed, I walked past broken-down corrals left from an aborted ranching venture. There was so little grass, it was hard to believe anyone had tried to ranch there. But hurricanes had altered this land since cattle grazed there; perhaps it had once been feasible. It was a long way across the sand and mud flats to the ponds.

The first ponds were disappointing, no ducks spotted their surface. But in the soil that had been dredged into piles I found a sandrose, a curious gray rock crystal nearly the size of a tennis ball. I cleaned the rose off and looked at its thousand facets. I held it so that the flat surfaces reflected, diamondlike, in the sunlight. The sandrose was clearly a good omen, and when I climbed to the top to the next soil pile to look at another pond, I saw, with binoculars, a single drake pintail paddling absently in the center. It was very much like I hoped it would be. He had been waiting for us, and I was sure he would be there in the morning.

I was back at the truck a little after noon. The sun had just begun to heat the top of the truck, but it was still cool inside. Dolly, Jake, and Spud were still comfortable. I eased the pickup back on the beach and headed toward the mainland. Now the beach was filling with tourists and fishermen. We passed a park ranger in a green pickup and I felt sure that I would not get caught if I flew Dolly early in the morning. Everything was set, one more flight at snipe and she would fly without jesses, bell, or radio. My migration was nearly finished; hers, perhaps, was about to begin.

We crossed the causeway and drove through Corpus Christi. Then we found a back road heading toward Bishop, and searched it for another flooded field with snipe and killdeer. It was three-thirty when we finally came across what we were looking for. I decided that if she caught a snipe I would let her eat it all. I would not weigh her again, she could regulate her own weight from now on.

When I took Dolly from the back of the pickup, the dogs did not seem interested. Perhaps they knew that their season was over. But when I removed Dolly's hood, she looked as keen and ready as I had ever seen her. The flesh around her eyes had turned a deep yellow, and her feathers were dusky with a rich bloom. She lifted off my fist with grace; in seconds she was fifty yards away, gaining speed and altitude. In a minute she was nearly out of my sight on the north horizon. Five minutes later she had crossed high above my head and nearly disappeared to the south.

And all the time she rose higher and higher, daring the snipe to make a break for cover. She was trying to make it seem as if she was not interested in killing a snipe, and for an instant I almost fell for the act and thought about calling her down to the lure. But I was alert enough not to be tricked. One of the snipe was not.

It broke from the relative safety of the water and flew uncertainly toward the road ditch. Dolly waited until it had gone too far to return before she started her stoop.

From where I stood, I could see that she would overtake him easily. Then I noticed the power poles along the road and the three wires stretched loosely between them. Dolly snatched the snipe neatly from the air but her follow-through sent her into the wires. Luckily she was not going full speed and had seen the wires in time to flare her wings, slowing even more. But the collision was still forceful. She dropped the snipe, tumbling from the sky as if she had been shot. I was stunned.

Then I began to run. It was a slow, clumsy one-hundred-yard dash that seemed to take forever. When I reached the place where Dolly had hit the wire, I stopped, closed my eyes for an instant, then looked over the fence where I had seen her tumble. She stood in the field, alive but hurt. Her left wing drooped and her dark eyes were dull. Then she hopped toward me and I knelt to take her up on my fist. She barked defiantly at me as if to prove that she was still a peregrine. But there was no denying the fact that she could not fly, that her migration, and mine, was ended.

I sat by the fire at my camp watching the driftwood's blue flames and thought of Icarus. Poor foolish Icarus. The sun had set hours before and the dogs had been fed. Already I had checked on Dolly a dozen times. She seemed content on her perch in the back of the truck. Her wing was not broken, and there was only a little bleeding where the wire had torn the skin. But it was sore; she held it low. It would be stiff for several days at least. Had she hit the wire a day later, she would have starved to death before the wing healed.

I held each piece of driftwood tightly in my hands before I fed it to the fire. It was impossible for me to touch the wood without thinking about where it had traveled, where it had once been alive and green. The jungles of the Yucatan, Belize, and Brazil came to mind. They were places Dolly might have seen. I wondered if the wood had fallen in a windstorm and been washed out to sea; or if it had been cut by men, used as part of a boat or a packing crate before it washed up on the beach. I smelled the wood and imagined the richness of the lands I would never see. I smelled exotic fruit, spices, and kelp.

And sometime after midnight, the wind came up and I moved closer to the flames. We would be leaving in the morning, headed for the Black Hills. After nearly four months and five thousand miles of driving, we were finished. And though finally I had failed, it had not been all a loss. A thin strand of steel had decided Dolly's fate. That was one thing I did not have to worry about. But in the next day or two, I would have to make some decisions about myself. The wind that had come up reminded me of everything that was north of me: mountains, grasslands, the little ranch on the edge of the Black Hills, and Kris. But I had a good two days of driving to think about what I would do. There was time.

The night passed quickly. I watched the lights of ships in the Gulf moving toward places that I had only dreamed of. I made note of the way the constellations rode the sky at different angles above this final camp. At last dawn came and the stars and ships seemed to disappear. I began walking when it was still too dark to insure good footing but, just before I reached the pond where the pintail had been, the sun came up. The sky would be prairie-blue today. The wind began to swing and soon there was a sea breeze coming steadily against my face. It carried the smells that I had found in the driftwood the night before.

In the night, the old drake had been joined by a half dozen other ducks. As I moved toward the pond, they swam out from the bank toward the center. I froze and watched them, marveled at their colors and the smooth curve of their necks. These were northern ducks, raised on the potholes of the high plains, and even though some of them could have been birds of the year, it was as if they had used this pond before. These ducks knew this place and I couldn't help thinking that they knew me too. Certainly the old drake knew me. He had been waiting.

The hens quacked to each other and I saw the drake twist his elegant head and look skyward. He did not believe I had come alone. But when I took one more step, he lifted from the pond with the others. They circled, staying close to the water, not wanting to fly over the land. They whistled past me, and made one more revolution of the pond. The old drake eyed me as they passed. He craned his neck and looked at me as if to say that he knew she was up there, out of his vision, waiting to fold on them as they left the pond. I took a few more steps and they broke away over the land. They flew tentatively at first, but when the roar of the stoop did not come, they gained confidence and lined out. The old drake stayed low, hugging the contour of the earth where he was safest. But he knew, as I had come to know, that he was never truly safe from a peregrine. He knew that the height of the falcon's pitch is hard to judge and that the higher the pitch, the more irresistible the stoop.

I watched the pintails until they were specks on the horizon. One speck remained closer to the ground than the rest. It was the old drake, who believed Dolly was still above him. I wanted to believe he was right, that she was simply too high to see. I turned and started back to the pickup. As I walked, I imagined her still above the ducks, still above me, pumping from horizon to horizon, with a view of everything below. I imagined her careening through the thinnest of air, retaining only the slightest connection to earth, so very high that she blended with my dreams.

EPILOGUE

*N*ow I spend my time on the ranch in South Dakota. Dolly will live the rest of her life in a large airy chamber, with padded perches and a view of the Black Hills. Kris goes to work at the regional hospital in Rapid City every morning before it is light and keeps men and women alive while the surgeons repair their hearts. Spud has grown up. Jake is dead.

Dolly's mature plumage is a dusky slate blue on her back with horizontal black spots on her breast. Her wing has healed completely, but the brightness has never fully returned to her eyes. It is clear to us all that she will never be a wild bird. Now she only flies for a few months each year when Erney and I bring her out to hunt the local ducks and grouse. She has already had one more chance at being wild and free than is reasonable to expect. Both times the hazards proved too much. Sometimes I see injustice in what happened to her. Sometimes I want to say that the eagle in Montana was a natural hazard, but the power line in Texas was unnatural, man-made, and so unfair. But I am not so sure.

From time to time I believe I have become wiser. Usually I feel I have learned nothing.

Now, when the first cold wind of autumn presses down on the ranch house and forces itself through the cracks between the windows and the sills, I have an idea where it has been and where it is going. But I don't know if the whine it makes in the cottonwood leaves is meant for me. When the first cold front of winter touches me, a chill runs down my back and I can see the birds in my mind. I can feel the ducks begin to fidget on their prairie ponds. I know that they will all be moving soon but I still don't know what it all means or how it really works.

And, when I see the north wind pushing the prairie grass in front of it, I know that it is pushing peregrines too. I know that peregrines are riding it southward. But not Dolly. And not me. We may catch a duck and cook it over an open fire. We may sleep outdoors and watch meteors streak through the belt of Orion. But we will be staying here. We will live out our lives in the center of the continent, surrounded by the movement of birds. We will remain lodged between the greens and browns of the earth and the endless blue of the prairie sky.

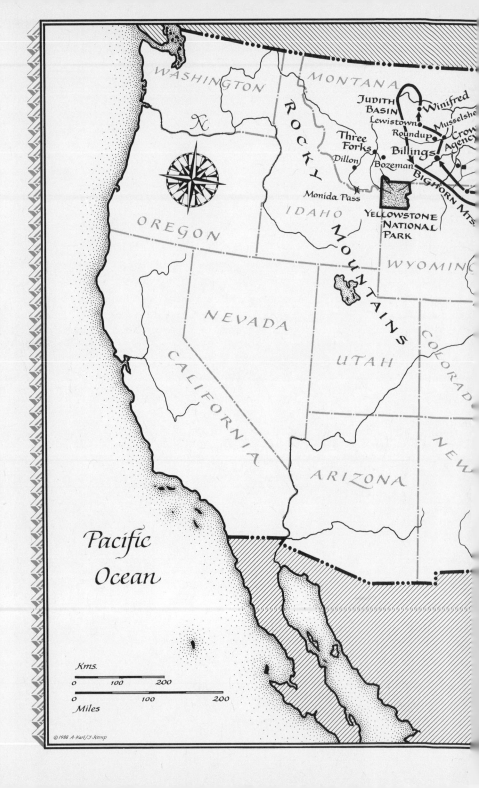

WASHINGTON

MONTANA

JUDITH
BASIN
Winifred
Lewistown
Musselshe
Roundup
Three
Forks
Billings
Crow
Agency
Dillon
Bozeman
BIGHORN Mts.
Monida Pass
ROCKY

IDAHO

YELLOWSTONE
NATIONAL
PARK

OREGON

WYOMING

MOUNTAINS

NEVADA

UTAH

COLORAD

CALIFORNIA

NEW

ARIZONA

Pacific
Ocean

Kms.
0   100   200

0   100   200
Miles

© 1988 A·Karl / J·Kemp